100 DAYS OF BRAVE

How to launch a business you love in three months

Iolanthe Gabrie

MAJOR
STREET

For Yule and Eglé

 First published in 2022 by Major Street Publishing Pty Ltd
info@majorstreet.com.au | +61 421 707 983 | majorstreet.com.au

© Iolanthe Gabrie 2022
The moral rights of the author have been asserted.

 A catalogue record for this book is available
from the National Library of Australia

Printed book ISBN: 978-1-922611-40-6
Ebook ISBN: 978-1-922611-41-3

Cover design by Tess McCabe
Internal design by Production Works

10 9 8 7 6 5 4 3 2 1

Contents

PART TWO
Building Brave

PART THREE
Being Brave

Preface

Can you be brave, just for today?

Within the answer to this one little question lies the key to your freedom.

You may have picked up my book because you want to build a successful business and you'd like a practical, clear guide for doing so. That's terrific. *100 Days of Brave* will certainly help get you there. But while this book is about business, it's actually about something much bigger and more powerful than commerce: it's about living life on your own terms. It's about freedom. Building a successful business is one of the best ways to reclaim ownership of your life and identity, because it offers you the flexibility and creativity our patriarchal society's structures and norms routinely deny us. And by 'us', yes – I am referring to women. You're the focus of *100 Days of Brave*; you're the community I want to empower and embolden with business strategy so you can enjoy lives in deep connection with your soul.

This isn't to say that men won't find utility in this book. You fellas will, too: my plan offers you 100% business gold and roaring momentum. But it's women I've written this book for, as it's women who are under the double burden of a fantasy our Western community has foisted upon us. You know the one I'm talking about: the dirty fantasy that YOU CAN DO IT ALL.

I went to a prestigious private girls' school with a focus on academic integrity and grrrlll power, '90s style. In an era of Spice Girls feminism, the environment I was raised in demanded excellence and the astronomical marks to attend Australia's version of an Ivy League university. From there, we could be anything we wanted: lawyers, doctors, lawyers. (Did I mention lawyers twice? Oops, I'm sorry. It really was drilled into us!) We could be wives and mothers, too, at an appropriate time (somewhere between the ages of 28 and 31, give or take – any earlier and you were an unfortunate; any later, at the risk of spinsterhood and infertility). Like my girlfriends, I wanted to succeed academically. While I mistakenly thought being an academic would be the route I'd take, many of my friends wanted careers in suits in large corporations. Winning careers in highly competitive (and often male-dominated) industries is still viewed as the coup de grâce for most privileged women.

The subtext to this fantasy is this: you've really made it once a large corporation has accepted you.

The behaviour you exhibit: behave as a man would to succeed within his world.

This kind of relentless career will be familiar to many of you reading this. It consists of gym-sessions at 5.30 a.m. to keep dat body right (because the relative size of your body correlates with your sense of discipline and control, naturally). It means being in the office at 7.30 a.m. – extra-large, extra-extra-strong long black in hand – to beat the boss. It means excruciatingly long hours and anxiety-inducing travel duties in a job that has become passionless (yet financially grows ever more lucrative the longer you're in the trenches). And it means dulling your worries and tiredness with a fat glass of red wine with 'the team' before you leave the office to go home at 7 p.m.

The reality: you're working for The Man.

And that's no way to freedom. Choose to work for the woman. (That's you, BTW.)

A life working for The Man is not very fulfilling. It's also unsustainable, as many of you will realise once the vagaries of the real world and your biology begin to knock upon your door. The dissonance between the kind of person you need to be to enjoy society's approval and the kind of person you ACTUALLY are results in what is becoming known as a quarter-life crisis. It hits women hard in particular, and it takes them out of the game in droves once they have children. That's because – despite lip-service to the contrary – women are generally still the heavy lifters when it comes to domestic life.

They cook the dinners, pack the lunches, buy the gifts, clean the house, clothe the children and arrange the logistics around school drop-offs and pick-ups. Simultaneously, they're also expected to take care of their aging parents, organising everything from geriatrician appointments to ensuring Nana is included in Christmas plans (even when she lives three hours away). And at work? At work, in order for her to be accepted by her male peers, she must arrive, leave and perform as if she had NONE of the domestic responsibilities she shoulders.

This taxing triple workload is the result of telling women, 'You can be anything you want', which ignores the persisting, barely veiled sexism in our communities and households. It's Western feminism at its most facile, delivered at half-term, unformed and unsupported by the power structures that drive our economy. It's a rigged game, a terrible double bind based on an awful lie: if you work hard enough, you'll be rewarded. You'll finally be allowed into the club.

Schools such as my own failed to tell their students that this club is owned by the boys, and you'll have to play by their rules to remain relevant. So, we're set up to fail, scaling corporate heights post–tertiary degrees, burning bright into our early 30s... before crashing out of 'serious business' if we have children, compromised by life's realities. Babies need feeding. Supermarkets need visiting, as do doctors and your parents, too. Women feel stretched and apologetic about having to negotiate flexible working hours with their employers. They accept roles that are less dynamic than they deserve, wrung out and shamed by the caring, the rearing, the feeding, the cleaning. Our domestic responsibilities are like some kind of dirty secret, not to be spoken about in corporate environs at the cost of our reputations. I call bullshit on the lie we've been told about the wide possibilities a woman's life presents and the structures we have allowed to hold us captive.

The book you are holding in your energised hands is a manifesto for women, a practical call to action. It's an invitation to live life on your own terms, and a guidebook for taking the first steps towards independence and creativity. Accepting this challenge means totally sidestepping the structures we're told give us social currency and forging an existence that suits the real life you lead, that makes pockets of time for your passions, your partner, your children and your parents. It means the end of apologising for who you are, what you are and your responsibilities.

It also means the beginning of hard work. For this quest, you will need to be brave.

Let's be real. Life is a mixture of ups and downs, challenges and victories. Don't spend life hiding from the difficulties coming your way – a scary, path-changing event is coming for all of us, sure as birth and death. You can't avoid the hard stuff. But you can CHOOSE your hard, which makes a fundamental difference in your journey through the gross-out. Choosing your hard doesn't remove life's stressors, nor does it guarantee plain sailing. But what it does guarantee is that you're in the driving seat of your destiny, moving full-crank into a future that reflects who you are 24-7. The painful war between the 'business' you and the actual you will no longer have the ammunition to be waged, because your bravery in choosing to live life on your own terms will give you a permanent passcard to living without apology.

I want this for you. You want this for you.

Women stepping into their power by choosing to live 24-7 lives of business, passion, family and self-care is the only true way to address gender inequality and the imbalance of power. This book gives you the roadmap to begin this process of realising your most fulfilling life by capitalising upon your strengths, your intelligence and your divine intuition. This intelligence lies within you already, waiting quietly for your energy and bravery to bring it to life. Mark my words: your business is the key that will unlock the door to freedom. It is the ultimate teacher. Business isn't just for men. It's not just for people with degrees, or those from money with fat overdrafts to support them through lean times. It's not just for white people. It's for EVERYONE.

There is no secret to success in business. There is only the choice to accept total responsibility for your life.

This is your moment to be brave.

Just for today.

If you can do that for me, together we can build your business and change the trajectory of your life.

With great love and support,

Iolanthe

Introduction

Finding your business course

Business is personal.

Many's the time I've heard the phrase, 'It's just business, it's not personal'. I've heard this from the lips of colleagues and friends explaining their reasons for making a choice between two service providers – be they real estate agents, house painters or nannies. This phrase is presented to the disappointed recipient as a form of kindness. In Western society, where polite obfuscation is our preference, this catch-all 'letting you down easy' phrase is used to hide all manner of useful conversations and practical feedback. The primary function of this lazy expression is to be a smokescreen against guilt: it protects the 'decider' from considering that maybe, just maybe, their decision-making process should be informed by more than the lowest price. Of course, we don't always deserve to win business – our offering might not match a client, or we might have a gap in our offering. In these cases, if we've put time and effort into presenting our service with care and intention, the least the would-be client should offer is a fair, transparent assessment of why we lost. Platitudes such as 'It's just business, it's not personal' do a great disservice to all of us.

I reject this lazy expression entirely. For me, business *is* personal. My business is an extension of me: it's my talents, my intentions and my focus made real. It's the lifeblood of my existence, giving me the energy I need to live in comfort and the resources I need to offer others meaningful work. My business is as personal to me as my child: it is my creation, and I am its mother.

I understand that for many of you, 'Business is personal' is a difficult notion to let into your heart. There's an emotional risk should your business be rejected, if you believe that you are your business. 100 Days of Brave is all about taking nervous steps into the big blue beyond, taking small sips of emotional risk like (empowering!) medicine each day – and in just over three months you WILL have a business and begin taking steps to living life on your own terms.

How does this idea sit with you? Do you believe that business is personal? What emotions does this bring up for you?

Let me tell you, the emotional risk of associating yourself with your business on the deepest level is worth it. That's because your business is about to become an additional member of your family, and without profound devotion and passion, it won't work. Your 100 Days of Brave might pass quickly, but not without consuming you, exciting you, frightening you, depressing you and emboldening you at one time or another. This life-changing journey you've chosen is a time for big emotions, connecting with intuition and committing to yourself.

On this journey, you will have people you never thought interested in you surprise you with their support and generosity. You will have the opportunity to reassess some of your closest friendships and familial ties. Some of the people who should be enthusiastic about your business will shut you down. Some of them might bring out the old chestnut, 'It's just business, it's not personal'. You might try to explain away the negative responses to your adventure into freedom and business. The reality is that people who question your capacity to have a business – or choose not to support your business when they really should – are being challenged by your rebirth. Just by holding this book in your hands, you are braver than many people who surround you – you're readying yourself to experience 100 Days of Brave, you badass.

So, here's how it works:

- **Brave Beginnings – Meeting Your Business:** Your first trimester is all about free-flowing imagination, looking for the business of your future in the clues of your past, connecting with your intuition, addressing gaps in the market, looking critically at your strengths and conducting research into the viability of your potential business. During this month, you decide upon your startup business; this is a time of dreams grounded in reality and market forces. Make no bones about it: you're about to become a business owner.

- **Building Brave – Bringing Your Business into Being:** Your second trimester is about the process of coaxing your business concept into being. It's such a cracking month! You'll be deciding on your business name, registering details with the relevant tax authorities (I promise you this is more exciting than it sounds), branding like a boss and legitimising your project. 100 Days of Brave isn't about creating naff businesses that are half-baked: your business will become a big, badassed, branded reality that others will RESPEKT.

- **Being Brave – Working in and on Your Business:** The last trimester is when you climb your Mount Everest. The 100 Days of Brave community and I will be here to celebrate your wins and support you through your challenges. Like birthing a real live babe, you're about to birth a real live business, babe. Same same, but different. During this period of time, you'll be working in your business, reaching out to potential customers, following them up and networking. Once you come out of this last trimester, you will be a business owner. I'm so excited for you and all the potential we're about to release!

This is what you'll need to make 100 Days of Brave work for you:

The will to be brave, just for today.

That's it.

Well, you'll also need an internet connection and an hour or so a day to work on your business with real focus. And I mean FOCUS – no Facebooking or distractions from your purpose.

If you've got the will and the wi-fi, I've got the way. Know that, as of right now, you are only 100 days away from having your business. How frickin' exciting is that?!

Support for the brave

Throughout the next three-and-a-bit months, I've got your back – and so does the 100 Days of Brave community. Here are a variety of ways to cheer your Brave journey on:

- Join the private **100 Days of Brave** Facebook Group for daily support.
- Use your **100 Days of Brave** Playbook to document your growth and achievements (100daysofbrave.com/resources).
- Book a one-on-one **100 Days of Brave** intensive session with me. (iolanthegabrie.com/contact).

Imagine yourself as Bilbo Baggins at the start of *The Hobbit*. Sure, you're a little nervous to be leaving Bag End, but you know there are wild adventures to be had away from the comfort of your hobbit-hole. The reward? Life on your own terms.

Go get it, girl.

Part One

Brave Beginnings

Meeting Your Business

Welcome to the beginning of your first trimester of 100 Days of Brave! How are you feeling? Excited? A bit nervous? Curious? Me too! While all three Parts of 100 Days of Brave are important, the first trimester is particularly critical because it forms the solid foundation your business is built upon.

You're about to journey into a state of ambiguity – a little like being in the first throes of a relationship, or those woozy hopeful weeks of anticipating pregnancy. It's a weird space to be in – there's a lot of hope, plenty of anticipation... and absolutely no guarantees of anything. Boil the kettle and make friends with ambiguity. Living life on your own terms means nothing is set in stone, but freedom is yours. Let's get started.

Research from the Australian Bureau of Statistics shows that 49% of Australian business startups fail within four years. The reasons for failure are various, with Australian Securities and Investments Commission statistics showing 40% had inadequate cash flow or high cash use. Some business ideas simply aren't sound, which speaks to a lack of research and enquiry on the entrepreneur's part. Other business owners think entrepreneurial spirit and Google alone will be enough to help them run a successful business.

No-one wants to fail, obviously. But nature alone shows us that not everything can work. The idea of 'failing forward' or 'failing fast' is a dominant one in the startup community. I have mixed feelings about the blokey gung-ho-ness of 'fast failing' – not because I disagree with the idea that it's better to cut your losses on a notion that's not working, but because having business concepts fail repeatedly comes at a financial and emotional cost. Avoiding failure in business is impossible, but working to establish a business prototype that has the likelihood of success is your goal in the coming month.

So be alert, but not alarmed. Be diligent, but don't be a downer.

Chapter 1

What's your why?

Why do you want to be in business?

There's no right answer to the question of why you want to be in business, but there's surely a wrong answer: money. If your core motivation to be in business is money, it's time to slow things down and take a deep breath.

I can completely understand why you may have thought about money as your key motivator first up: so much of the marketing around women and entrepreneurship is focused on ostentatious wealth, evinced in the form of sleek, aspirational Instagram feeds peppered with YSL clutches, diamond-clad hands clutching Starbucks coffee cups, and Valentino Rockstud pumps. As if these items were the signifiers of a successful businesswoman. As if they were the inevitable outcome of being in business. Let me tell you: it's a con.

It's not that I don't like money. I do, I love it. It affords me the gingerbread house I live in, my Obus splurges and the ability to Uber Eats to my heart's content. I respect and enjoy money. I set financial goals for my business and am absolutely elated when I achieve and exceed them. I have diamonds and fancy bags.

But money is not my business 'why'. It never was. My business 'why' is freedom and the ability to live life on my own terms doing something I'm proud of. I use my mind and my heart to create beautiful, meaningful words and images for others. I can be myself – it's my very me-ness that attracts people to my business. If money were my key motivator for being in business, I'd go and get a corporate job today. I would have done so many years ago.

If money is your 'why', you simply won't have enough reason to turn up each day when the going is tough, or boring, or stressful. If money is your 'why', the number of hours you put into your business versus your financial reward in the startup years will represent a crushing imbalance. Being in business can absolutely be a way to wealth, but it needs to be about more than wealth – philosophically, I don't think we can grow financially or emotionally rich if our goal is lucre alone.

BRAVE ACTIVITY: Let's work on your 'why'

Set aside 15 minutes to write down your answers to the following questions in a beautiful notebook, on your computer or in your 100 Days of Brave Playbook:

· Why do you want to be in business?
· What can business ownership offer you that being an employee cannot?
· If you were self-employed, what would your Monday look like?
· What do you value most in life?

Now answer again: why do you really want to be in business?

Chapter 2

What's your skill?

How can you be of service?

What can you do that fulfils a need? This question can be a real roadblock, and yet it must be answered to get the show on the road! Feeling a twinge of overwhelm, or a stab of imposter syndrome? Here's why: the entrepreneurs we are often encouraged to idealise – the Bransons, Jobses and Zuckerbergs of the world – have businesses that are unique. We admire them from a distance, what with their fully realised brands, mission statements and original products.

Yet each of these entrepreneurs fulfils a very basic need. Branson gets people around. Jobs made work easier. Zuckerberg collects data for marketers.

When I began my social media agency Ruby Assembly, I had no brand, but I did have a skill: I'm a great communicator, a gifted writer. I know that few people have this skill. Is my skill unique? No, there are other great communicators and writers out there. Does that mean I can't make my business as a communicator a rip-roaring success? HELL NO!

First things first: you do not have to reinvent the wheel to have a business. You do not have to create a whizz-bang new piece of technology or a medical cure (although that would be awesome) to feel worthy of entrepreneurship. It's a big world out there, and there's room for everyone to have a crack and make a profit. That's why people keep training to become electricians, hairdressers and accountants: as a society, we need their services. Do you have any preconceived notions around the word 'startup'? Because you're about to have one!

From my time in business incubators and coworking communities, 'startup' seems to be mysteriously applied only to technology concepts. I can't say why – maybe it's a macho Silicon Valley thing we've unconsciously adopted. A startup can be literally any business. From the kids' lemonade stand next door to a bookkeeping service, a dog-walking business to an app development service: if it is young and having a crack, it's a startup.

If you're having trouble thinking of a specific skill you have, try reflecting on what makes you feel in flow. Warning: woo-woo incoming! But you've already bought the book: in for a penny, in for a pound. Being in flow means something different to everyone – to me it means a kind of ease born from confident calm. It feels like you're in sync, like you're not working against the tide. It's when ideas come from the ether easily, and when work is deep without being stressful. Here are some examples of being in flow from my end, and the skill being used:

- When I'm in a meeting with clients and we've come up with an amazing, creative way to market their brand, I feel a deep, buzzing happiness. I'm totally comfortable, excited and elated in that space. Skills used: imagination, creativity and problem-solving.
- When I'm engaged as a speaker, sharing my story to an obviously receptive and happy audience, I feel in the right place, with useful information to share. Skills used: public speaking, clear expression and storytelling.
- When I'm writing a really juicy blog post that blows stereotypes about women and money out of the water, I feel like really robust

ideas are coming to me easily. Skills used: imagination, creativity and written communication.

BRAVE ACTIVITY: What's your skill?

Write down five skills you have. Don't be shy!

Set aside one hour across two days to write down your answers in a beautiful notebook, on your computer or in your 100 Days of Brave Playbook. Examples could include creativity, fine attention to detail or a beautiful phone manner. There's no wrong answer!

For each of these skills, write down three business concepts that have these skills at their heart. For example:

· **Creativity:** Styling corporate spaces to feel inspiring. Being an illustrator. Baking beautiful pies.
· **Fine attention to detail:** Outsourced administration. Make-up artist. Recruiter.
· **A beautiful phone manner:** Cold calling for other people. Bookkeeping. Running Airbnbs.

Now, write down five things that make you feel in flow, and then identify the skills you're using when in that state. For example: you feel calm and creative when baking. Skills used: attention to detail, creativity, and talent for making delicious food.

For each of these skills, write down three business concepts that have these skills at heart. For example, if you have a talent for making delicious food: cooking classes; nutritionist; pop-up coffee shop.

Now that you've clarified your skills and identified when you're in flow, look over the potential business concepts you've collated with a discerning eye. You should have a good bunch at your disposal! Highlight the ones that appeal to you most and let those ideas marinate.

Chapter 3

Your intuition

It will lead you in the right direction

It's entirely possible you've come to 100 Days of Brave with the beginnings of a business concept – or even a more fully-fledged notion you're champing at the bit to reveal to the public. That's awesome! Or, at this stage, you may still be trying on ideas for size – which is totally normal, too. Whatever stage you're at, it's important to be guided by your intuition.

Don't get me wrong: this doesn't mean joining a kundalini yoga squad or going on a juice cleanse to get in touch with yourself. The universe and the world surrounding us are tickling our intuition bone all the time. When I decided to leave academia behind and become a real estate agent, nothing rational was guiding my hand. Everyone was deadset against it, I had no true background in business, wasn't very good with maths and didn't know the first thing about real estate. What I did have was a strong sense that real estate was something I needed to try my hand at. This is an example of intuition in action. Equally, when I decided that real estate was no longer serving me, intuition persuaded me to pull the pin. I had no reason to do so and could have happily gone on for years selling property successfully – but I was being drawn to begin my own business.

It's important to make peace with the fact that your intuition will not always make sense in the moment. It might ask you to make unpopular choices (leaving that well-paid job, moving from the country to the city, getting a wild undercut) that you tussle with. It may encourage you to develop in areas that you have no logical reason to stray into. Today you could be a lawyer, but your intuition is guiding you towards life as a doula. Stranger things have happened!

The reason I want you to focus on cultivating a relationship with your intuition during your first trimester is because it's such an enormously powerful latent business ideation tool. You're in the throes of sifting and uncovering your future as a business owner. To help you come to a decision about the first business adventure you'll take – that initial step towards living life on your own terms – you need a whole arsenal of ideation tools. Tuning into intuition is key among them, so stick with me now.

Intuition is a bit like the artist's muse: sometimes you can see her clearly, and other times she's a barely visible blur at the back of your consciousness urging you to take action. Some of you will be more tuned in to your intuition, and others might be finding it harder to hear your inner guidance clearly. This can be particularly tricky when your intuition is encouraging you towards a business concept you know nothing about.

At its core, becoming a business owner is an act of faith in both yourself and the world around you. While we yearn to intellectualise the process of business development – indeed, this book is such a project – it's really about gut and grit. If this sounds scary, I urge you to remember how intuitive you are right now: having this powerful tool of a book in your hands is testament to this.

Feeling like you want to go deeper into your intuition? Clarify the messages of internal guidance you're receiving over the coming days. You might find some of the activities explained in the rest of this chapter become part of your weekly business practice!

Meditation

Meditation is celebrated ad nauseum because it is such an important tool for slowing down. Slowing down and having space between thoughts allows intuition to reveal itself to you as glimmers of information. I regularly practice meditation to alleviate stress, nod off to sleep and quiet my mind. I'm not a particularly Zen individual, but I know that meditation has helped to lower my anxiety and refresh my mind, and that's good enough for me.

I recommend setting aside ten to fifteen minutes per day to meditate.

You could meditate before you go to sleep, or first thing in the morning – or any damn time, actually, just so long as you do it and observe how you feel afterwards. Don't overthink the process and feel you're failing if you can't quiet your mind, or if you don't have an amazing business concept pop into your noggin fully realised. Just give it a crack and see if it offers any new capacity for insight at this important juncture in your business development.

Use a meditation app. Don't go it alone with guidebooks or subject yourself to hardcore meditation bootcamps. This is about ease and effective use of time, not becoming a guru. These are two of my favourite meditation apps:

- **Headspace:** A beautiful app to use, Headspace features a variety of meditation offerings, including a free set on the foundations of meditation. It earns bonus points for its practical, non-woo-woo interface and charming host.
- **Calm:** A beautiful app with free offerings, Calm has breathing exercises, guided meditations and beautiful sleep stories to send you off to the land of nod. Divine!

Return to your body

If you're a businessperson (which you are, by the way), you are likely to have lots of terrific ideas spinning around in your noggin. On top of these, you've got responsibilities to others, a shopping list, Netflix binges to indulge in and a bundle of other things on your mind. Here's the thing: we're in our minds too much. While our brains are wonderful, magical helpers, they are only part of our intuitive story. When we overload them with media, responsibilities, ideas and excitement – and tire them out with coffee, wine, fatty foods and too many late nights – they are not always the most reliable source of information.

That's why having the opportunity to return to bodily intuition is so important. Your body will always tell you what's up: you've just gotta learn to tune into her. She's a true manifestation of intuition, tugging you towards some things (rest, play, your awesome new business) and away from others (toxic people, places with weird energy). Sitting within your body and cultivating an awareness of what the body wants you to know is a commitment. It's particularly useful during 100 Days of Brave because you're downloading so much information about your new life, and your body will help guide your intuition, helping you to make better decisions.

Here are a few ways I return to my body each week:

- **Yoga and dance:** I'm fortunate to attend a beautiful gym in Melbourne's inner north. It's more of a movement studio, and you won't find a protein shake in sight. I start and end my weeks with a blissful hour of Slow Flow yoga to stretch stuff out, let stuff go and really be in my body. I also love dance classes and get down to YouTuber The Fitness Marshall to work up a sweat and shake out the bad juju.

- **Reiki and massage:** Every few weeks I enjoy a massage and reiki session with a beautiful healer. I can feel my body releasing pent-up stress and softening under her touch. She's also a pseudo counsellor, and she encourages me to be kind to myself. We can all do with a bit more of that in our lives, I'd say. I've also undertaken a course in reiki, and I will give myself reiki before bed or when I'm feeling like I need to heal and be inside my body. For those who haven't experienced reiki, it is a gentle, powerful mode of energetic healing many people find soothing, relaxing and replenishing.
- **Walking:** Being in nature and gently strolling is a great way to connect with the environment around you. If you can, try walking without listening to a podcast or music. I personally find this tricky, as I love learning and grooving along to sweet tunes, but know more information and staying in my brain won't reconnect me to my body. Observe the trees, people, footpaths and scenery as you pass by. Feel the weight of your body in your feet and reconnect.
- **Cooking:** A totally immersive experience, cooking engages all the senses. It brings you back to your body in the touching of produce, the slow method of preparing a delicious meal. Of course, it nourishes you too!
- **Bathing:** If you're lucky enough to own a bath, go for a soak with a good handful or two of salts. Even a shower can reconnect you to your physicality. If I'm feeling really 'cooked', I find that spending a bit of time in water reminds me who I am again.
- **Working with moon cycles:** The woo-woo water is warm – jump on in! I have benefited from working with Dr Ezzie Spencer's book *Lunar Abundance*, which is a practical guide to engaging in Yin (being) and Yang (doing) over the course of a month. Whether or not you feel the moon is influential in your life,

a focus on both rest and action is critical to an entrepreneur's success and longevity. New moon and full moon sequences ask you to tune directly into both your body and your intuition, which is key to the process of Brave Beginnings.

Oracles

I love angel cards, tarot cards and oracle cards. I know they're not for everyone. I don't look to oracle cards as a way of answering exact questions about the future; for me, they're more like a think piece I will use for considering an opportunity, a problem or an idea. Oracle cards, by their very nature, engage your intuition muscle, asking you to interpret visual symbols and guidance in a way that matches your situation. I don't use them all the time, but I have found building a relationship with them most excellent: they always offer good advice and a fresh perspective.

If you feel drawn to oracle cards, try giving yourself a reading once a week for the first trimester. Here are some great resources to start with:

- **Download a virtual oracle card set:** Not ready to invest in a pack of cards yourself, or want to have a reading right here, right now? Go to your phone's app store and peruse Hay House's free oracle card offerings. They work in exactly the same way as the physical set (that is, the principle of the oracle card is that you draw energetically the cards you require) and form a nice introduction to the practice.
- **Recommended sets:** Some of my favourite card sets come from Rebecca Campbell, Danielle Noel, Kyle Gray and Lucy Cavendish. You can find card sets online at Booktopia or at any good purveyor of woo-woo goods.

BRAVE ACTIVITY: A week of cultivating intuition

Set aside half an hour each day this week to engage with your intuition through meditation, returning to your body, and using divination tools. Note how you feel before and after your intuition exercises in a beautiful notebook, on your computer or in your 100 Days of Brave Playbook. Note the ideas that come to you about your business during this time.

Tuning in to yourself, to intuition and to the wisdom circling around you are all forms of play. You may have some experience with these exercises, or you could be a total newbie to woo-woo. Whether you're a cynic or a card-carrying Angel Intuitive, have fun with these intuition tools and observe what you learn from the process of playing with each.

Chapter 4

Do your market research

Because not all business is good business

Just because I'm into woo-woo and taking cues from the universe doesn't mean I make business decisions on gut feeling alone (let alone angel cards). Over the last decade I've had the pleasure of spending time in many different business environments, including coworking spaces. In this time, I've observed many, many women (and blokes) going through the process of startup. With the rise of online and tertiary courses in what is now popularly called 'entrepreneurship', we are being presented with the possibility of an Instagram-curated life as a digital nomad, a mumpreneur or dadpreneur. Subsequently, many of the individuals I've observed going through startup are offering their services as coaches – a kind of catch-all phrase that means as much (and as little) as 'consultant'. In truth, I can count on one hand the women who've succeeded as coaches.

This is not to cast doubt on your career as a coach or consultant; it's merely a wake-up call to look beyond the 'You can do it' boss-chick-girlboss-mumpreneur-wyldtribe-nomad business communities you might frequent and work out if your business is truly viable as a marketable concept. Investigate the validity of your business offering, and don't fall into the trap of 'Just dream it, just believe it,' as touted by so many online business gurus and sycophantic Facebook Groups. So many potentially excellent businesspeople are encouraged into entrepreneurship, high on a social-media-fuelled hybrid of self-esteem quotes, online courses in funnel sales and a sprinkling of startup philosophy, applied wholesale onto any venture without enquiry. By not testing the validity of their business concept, they are unprepared for harsh market realities, which can lead to failure. By going into business without regard for the competitive environment you're entering, touting a generic offering – for example, as a nondescript coach or consultant – you're risking a lot.

Sure, there's the risk of losing some money and time – but more critically, you're at risk of losing your enthusiasm for entrepreneurship. Remember the idea of failing fast we discussed earlier? If we fail – and we burn out hard while we're high on the notion that passion alone will determine our success – there's a heavy psychological cost to pay. It's a bit like being in love for the first time. That first heartbreak is earth-shattering. It breaks our ideals and remakes us, wide awake to the realities of relationships: they're imperfect, and they don't always work.

Thankfully, biology and a desire for companionship usually see us seeking out new relationships after we've recovered. Not so with all business failure, however. When you fail at business from a position of wishful naivety – thinking that the market will support you whatever your offering, however flooded the market, because the world owes you, goddammit – you can fall so hard and take the rejection so personally that considering entrepreneurship a second time becomes an impossibility. I don't want you to ever feel that way about being an entrepreneur and living life on your own terms. Failure, whether of your business or just of a particular part of your offering, is normal in commerce. It's natural. How you deal with changing your business or amending your service – the resilience you cultivate and the attitude you bring upon entry into self-employment – makes all the difference to your longevity.

Avoid the risk of falling hard by getting in there and doing the hard work of testing your premise.

Statistics

Nothing throws a bit of perspective on a business like some cold, hard industry facts. Luckily, the Australian Bureau of Statistics does a fine job of researching industry trends on our behalf, so visit their website and take note of those critical numbers. Don't make your decision on these numbers alone – just use them for context and a sense of how many players are in your space. Do take note if you're investing in a category that is shrinking. A category shrinking can actually be an opportunity for you if you're bringing something new to it or paring it down to its essentials. Dig around. Why is it shrinking? What is replacing it? Is your business concept serving a group of consumers that is decreasing?

Conversely, if your category is exploding with demand, explore consumer motivation. Why does the public want such a service? Is it a novelty, or does the offering have longevity? You want your business to be an Uber, rather than a Pokémon GO. Consider market saturation and your point of difference once you've got the hard numbers at hand. I used to hate numbers, as I was forced to interact with them in an abstract way during high school. Being told there was only a single answer to an equation infuriated me! Now I relish numbers, as I use them to inform myself about a market or present compelling narratives based on statistics. Numbers are rubbery, of course, and you can coax them into whatever form you like. This activity is about informing yourself, though, so don't shape the stats to suit your wishful thinking! Be honest about what you discover, and appraise your business concept earnestly when you're empowered by this knowledge.

Poll the public

One of the biggest mistakes entrepreneurs make is failing to ask the public if they'd pay for their service or product. It's endemic across the startup community, and I can understand why: you're so buzzed about your amazing new business offering and the lifestyle it entails that you don't want to hear from the naysayers. You just want to get your website up, take your seat in the swanky coworking space and begin making money. You're totally convinced your idea is a winner. Hopefully it is – but don't you want to make doubly sure you've got a market before you go investing oodles of time, money and emotion into a business no-one wants? Yes, you do.

So, get polling. There are a variety of ways of doing this. Word to the wise: don't use a test group of your relatives or close friends. They care for you and are likely to respond positively out of obligation. What you need is candid feedback that will help you decide upon your most robust business concept. You'll find that real market feedback can help you build a better product or concept faster. Their feedback might even help you identify a gap in market to exploit! So, how to poll?

SurveyMonkey

SurveyMonkey is a powerful tool that allows you to create comprehensive questionnaires and surveys before sharing them with your networks via email, newsletters or social media. Easy to use for you and your audience, SurveyMonkey offers instant feedback in a format that's clear to interpret. When using SurveyMonkey, your feedback will only be as good as the questions you craft, however. Here are a couple of examples:

- **Useful question:** 'How do you feel when you need to let someone on your team go? What support would you benefit from at such a time?' This open-ended set of questions leaves room for your audience to express their needs.
- **Less useful question:** 'Would you lease your backyard?' This is a yes/no question, which doesn't give the audience any real context around leasing their backyard. However they answer, you have no insight into their decision-making process.

Share your SurveyMonkey with any Facebook Groups you're part of, send it to any existing databases you have access to, and make sure you post it in the 100 Days of Brave Facebook Group! As a community, we're here to support one another with real-talk feedback. SurveyMonkey also offers market research assistance and access to polling audiences, which you may find valuable.

Vox pop

It's time to bump shoulders with the great unwashed in the name of research! I'm sure that the idea of a vox pop has sent some of your hearts fluttering: 'Does she mean I need to go and speak to the public?' Yes, that's exactly it. Because of our interactions with insistent 'charity muggers', many of us feel worried that quizzing the general public about your business offering will be met with resistance and even abuse. While that's a possibility, it's really quite an unlikely one. Also, learning to speak to people 'cold' is an essential business skill that you'll need to build at some point – so, why not start building it this week?

When you're asking the public for feedback, make it snappy! From your SurveyMonkey poll, choose just three powerful questions to ask live subjects on the street. Go for ones that require the respondent to give you an answer of more depth than a simple yes or no.

There are a couple of good places to get your vox pop on. I recommend both, although you might initially feel more relaxed quizzing randoms in the latter:

- **Village people:** Go to a shopping village. Whether that's in the middle of the city or just the local supermarket, start there.
- **Industry forum:** Is there a business expo coming up that interests you? Will others from your industry or general field be in attendance? Try your vox pop questions there, too, and you'll benefit from a whole set of different responses to the answers your 'village people' offered.

It might take you a few goes to get your patter down and to feel more comfortable asking questions of the public. Give yourself two periods of half an hour each to poll the public at a couple of locations – you don't need to make it a day-long adventure. Importantly, don't take any rejections to heart. Most people are pretty friendly once they realise you're not after their wallets, stealing their time or guilting them about global injustice. Have a stack of choccies on hand to show your appreciation to subjects – and if you feel particularly cheeky, try and nab their email address to update them on your startup's progress!

BRAVE ACTIVITY: A week of resourcing

Put yourself at a competitive advantage by doing a deep dive into the viability of your business. Choose your top three business concepts and test them with as much rigour as you can muster. This process will stop you from investing your entire life savings into an ear candling business that sounded good in theory but just grossed people out in practice. By investing time in some basic market research, you'll enhance your chances of choosing a winning concept from the get-go.

Set aside around half an hour of each day per week to participate in each form of market research. Collate your subjects' responses to your business offering in a beautiful notebook, in a spreadsheet on your computer, or in your 100 Days of Brave Playbook. Make four feedback columns for each business concept you're considering: 'Pros', 'Cons', 'Objections' and 'Opportunities'.

Taking feedback and discoveries about your offering into account, which of the three business concepts you've tested is the most robust? Write this down concisely, as the process of explanation and justification is revelatory in itself!

Chapter 5

Observe your competition

There's room for everyone

Let's talk about your competition and the marketplace. How does the concept of your competitors make you feel? Do you avert your gaze and feign disinterest? Perhaps you are fascinated by your competition and pore over their every Instagram and website update. Maybe the idea of competition sets your teeth on edge with anxiety, setting your latent imposter syndrome abuzz. Alternatively, your offering may be so unique that you feel there is no true competition. I think I've had all of these emotions at one point or another when looking at others in the social media and digital strategy space I inhabit. And while fixing your attention on competition isn't something I feel you should do obsessively – in fact, it can be paralysing and destructive to your creativity in the long run – during this first trimester, tuning in to the marketplace is terrifically educative.

Before you begin your competition reconnaissance, I want you to understand that this is not an exercise in minimising your offering or diminishing your enthusiasm for your business concept. In the glossy, gorgeous world of digital, it's easy to compare your startup newbie model with the asset of a competitor who might be years into their business development. It may have taken your competitor years to resource themselves with the funds to make that digital identity as bodacious as you find it today.

Observing your competition is a lot like standing at the foot of several tall, beautiful mountains. Don't let the height of the things terrify you. They didn't appear overnight. You can't climb one in a day. Make your peace with that, and instead observe the qualities of each of the competitor-mountains. Some are dark and craggy, and you won't like what they represent. That's OK: take note of what you don't like about that mountain – there's rich knowledge in this process, revealing your own business values in sharp relief. Others will be bathed in a halo of influencer-angels and FIJI Water streams, precipitated upon by thousands of followers. They are the proverbial popular-girl mountains. Take note of what attracts you to those mountains and what similarities your business might have to them.

Business is intensely personal, and we all like to think our ideas are utterly unique. Of course, it's unlikely they are – which doesn't make them any less valuable. However, the process of observing your competition can be akin to putting on jeans that are too tight. You might feel uncomfortable and anxious. You might go into a momentary vortex of doubt about the value of your business concept, or feel like your market has been captured and that you'll never fit into those skinny jeans again.

My hint is this: buy new jeans, turn down the volume on the doubt without pretending it doesn't exist and keep on moving through the competition observation process. If you have a sound business con-cept, there is room for you in the market. How else do you imagine so many hairdressers, lawyers, fish and chipperies, and copywriters exist in the same space-time continuum? No two are alike, even though they ostensibly deliver the same service. It's a big world out there, made bigger courtesy of globalistion and the possibility of working with customers both locally and internationally. In the next trimester, you'll have the chance to work on differentiating your offering with marketing and content, which is not only bundles of fun but key to setting your business apart from the competition. Resist coming to this observation process with a sense of not being good or original enough: there really is room for everyone, you included.

BRAVE ACTIVITY: Watching mountains move

Set aside three hours to observe your competition for each of the business concepts you're considering. This should be ample time for you to look with some focus at six competitors. The internet makes this research process a relatively easy task. In a beautiful notebook, on your computer or in your 100 Days of Brave Playbook, create a document for each competitor with space for you to detail their offering, your emotional response to their brand, their audience, their point of difference and their marketing strategy. Note too how their offering is similar or different to your own. Are there any opportunities or weaknesses in their strategy that you can exploit to further refine your own business concept?

Here are some helpful questions for diving deeper into your observations:

- **What's their offering?** Take notes on their hero services or products. Are there any truly unique trademarked items in the mix? Are they collaborating with any other brands or businesses?
- **What's your emotional response?** Our purchasing decisions are rarely made solely by reason alone. When you look at the brand's website, Instagram feed or any other collateral they have available (such as ebooks and newsletters), how does it make you feel? Do you want in on their brand, or does it irritate you? If it irritates

you, why? Is it the branding presentation, an ethical qualm, or something else? Note how their audience is interacting with the business. Is there much conversation? What tenor does it have, and how does the brand respond? Would you consider them an accountable business or an unavailable business?

· **Who are their people?** Businesses create tribes. Looking at the brand's social suite, who would you identify as your competitor's tribes? Are they different or similar to your own? Get specific – you can even create groups to help you better understand audiences, such as 'Prue and Trudes' (middle-class, affluent, conservative dames) or 'Jonquil the Vegan' (socially aware and sustainability-minded). Have a bit of fun – life's too short!

· **What's their point of difference?** Do they have one differentiating factor that sets them apart? This could be an offering or an attitude, a visual device or cool branding. Note it down.

· **What's their marketing strategy?** How do they present their brand to the market? Do they provide heaps of information, or very little? Have you noticed their brand stalking you digitally after you visited their website? Note how they're tracking your behaviour as a potential customer. Do they offer freebies or add value? Do they have price schedules online, or nothing at all? Is there a 'loss leader' product they use to draw people in?

· **How does your offering differ from theirs?** Is theirs eco-focused? Is your pricepoint different? Think about all the ways your offering might be different (or similar) to theirs. Don't be dismayed if you feel that someone has already created 'your product'. Remember: there's room for everyone if you've got a solid business concept and a will to live life on your own terms!

After you've completed this exercise, which business concept are you most attracted to pursuing?

Chapter 6

Hack it

Immerse yourself in startup culture

Prior to writing this book, I participated in the world's biggest female hackathon, called #SheHacks. A hackathon empowers you to build a business in a weekend. Literally, a whole business, with a website, branding and strategy – the whole kit and caboodle in just over two days. Hackathons are usually associated with geeks tapping on their computers late into the night, fuelled by cold pizza and lukewarm beer. A product of the traditionally bloke-heavy Silicon Valley startup culture, hackathons often left women feeling excluded. Who wanted to spend three days holed up with odorous dudes late into the night, hunched over a laptop? Girl Geek Academy now runs #SheHacks events, which are fuelled by tea, cupcakes, snacks, yoga and making new friends. Doesn't that sound like a good way to get your business mojo on?

Here's how a hackathon works. On a Friday evening, you'll arrive at your hackathon venue. They're often coworking spaces, which offer you a neat insight into where the self-employed build their businesses on a daily basis. After an overview of the coming days from the event's organisers, you'll be paired with your teammates based on the skills you bring to the hackathon. You might be a great marketer and copywriter, a code-wily geek or a talented graphic designer. In many cases, you'll be mentored and offered additional research tools to fast-track your business concept. In collaboration with your teammates, you'll spend the following two days workshopping a concept, polling an audience and building a prototype minimum viable product. You may even have the chance to present your concept to a panel of angel investors. And just like that, when your powers combine, you've got the ability to build a business in a weekend!

Participating in a hackathon is not a prerequisite of completing your first trimester. They may only be held in your city once or twice a year. If you do have the chance to go hacking, I recommend you grab the chance with both hands. Here's what you'll get from a hackathon:

- You'll find a supportive environment that encourages you to put your skills to the test.
- You'll foster connection with a community of other talented, business-focused individuals with skills complementary to your own. You might very well meet your co-founders at a hackathon.
- You'll develop a working prototype or minimum viable product. This is the foundation you can then choose to pursue and polish as a team of entrepreneurs.
- You'll receive real-time constructive feedback on your product.
- You'll have the opportunity to present your business case to a panel of judges or angel investors.

Here's what you won't get from a hackathon:

- You can't guarantee that your business concept will be the one your team decides to pursue for the hackathon. Consider if you want to test your business idea in this space, or if you'd prefer to enjoy the business-building adventure and apply your new skills to your business concept afterwards.

- You might not develop a business idea with your team that you want to pursue. That's OK – it's about the process as much as the product.

BRAVE ACTIVITY: Find your hackathon

Spend half an hour or so researching local hackathons in your city and list them in a beautiful notebook, on your computer or in your 100 Days of Brave Playbook. Don't be discouraged from attending hackathons that aren't focused on female-run startups – while #SheHacks was an all-female weekend of big fun, hackathons with fellas in attendance are also terrific opportunities to immerse yourself in startup culture.

Chapter 7

Clarify your offering

You can't be all things to all people

Can you recall a time when you felt at the end of your tether? Tired out, strung out and freaked out? I'll bet you that these feelings came as the result of overcommitting yourself to others' needs. No shame: I've been there too. Obligations at work, to family, to our partners and our communities can have us coming last on the priorities list. One of the most transformative aspects of running your own business is a new-found consciousness about the way you're spending your time. As a former people-pleaser, I found myself saying 'yes' to event after event and job after job. I wasn't really considering if I truly wanted to attend these events, or if I took pleasure in the jobs I committed to. Obligation and saying 'yes' to business came first. At the heart of this behaviour – which many of us share and is often a default for women – is a scarcity mentality. We're motivated by disapproval rather than pleasure, worried that if people are offended, disappointed or rejected by us that work and love will dry up.

To this day, prioritising my own needs and interests remains a struggle. But I've learned – intellectually, at least – that I can't be all things to all people, even if I want to be! Because there are only so many hours in a day, and there's only so much me to go around. In

#girlboss startup culture, cute quips such as 'You have as many hours in the day as Beyoncé' are regrammed with abandon. These aphorisms are meant to inspire us by showing that if we only work hard enough, if we only chant our affirmations loud enough, we can have everything we want. Beware the pithy quote that guilts you into putting your own needs second. While you may share the same space-time continuum as Beyoncé, your own daily lived experience and hers are not the same. Beyoncé has the resources to curate an Instagram-perfect life – it's one of her products and something she invests in. Her efforts are amplified by a huge company of talented individuals. She isn't doing it all by herself, and she's not caring for three beautiful babies and creating groundbreaking feminist think pieces without support. My point is, you won't be more prodigious in your business by sacrificing yourself on the altar of productivity.

One discovery I made after I decided to be a businesswoman and live life on my own terms is that it irritated some people – some who were very close to me. It was as if the way I had chosen to divert my life's path disturbed and disappointed them. This was painful on all fronts. I find that relationships, particularly intimate female ones, can rupture at such times of redefinition – the big sliding-doors moments that happen in our lives and those of our companions, such as first boyfriends, engagements, weddings and babies. First businesses can easily be counted among these stressors.

My new identity as a business owner forced me to create new boundaries – and, more importantly, new priorities. Some friendships and behaviours I previously engaged in were no longer as important as my own life's goals. And I needed to clarify my new position to family and friends: yes, I still loved them. No, I wouldn't be going to every birthday event. I certainly wanted to catch up with them. But no, I wasn't up for a four-day, wine-fuelled girls' weekend. It just wasn't me anymore. In nearly every case, the clarification process around my new priorities occurred organically and my relationships adjusted with relative ease. In a couple of cases, things fell apart. And although that was a very painful and foreign experience (as anyone who has broken up with a female friend will know!), it was necessary. I couldn't continue to prioritise other people's needs ahead of my own. I had clarified my values, and in doing so made room for new relationships and improved relationships.

Exactly the same process applies when it comes to your business offering.

The more you bend over backwards trying to accommodate every client, every kind of payment, every project and timeframe that comes your way, the less focus and success your business will have. There is a terrific power in defining what you'll say 'yes' to and what you'll say a firm, grateful 'no' to. It is absolutely true that not everyone will love your offering – you won't be the right fit for everyone. This might feel frustrating, but it's no judgement upon you: sometimes clients are drawn to a business or provider because they like them more. There's no reasoning with gut feelings; we can only ever be who we are. This is yet another reason to feel confident in the market: there's room for everyone to thrive because our individual business offering cannot possibly be everything to everyone! Just as your offering will be the ideal solution for some clients, it will be unappealing to others. This is an empowering realisation that gives you the confidence to build an offering and marketing strategy that is founded in clarity.

Don't be a 'slashie'

In my experience as a business mentor and collaborative partner, I've found that clarity around their offering is the issue most entrepreneurs struggle with. In a global economy without boundaries or set working hours, we have the opportunity to be anything. Entrepreneurs are, by their nature, curious and exploratory creatures: they will often have a wide background of experience and knowledge to draw upon by the time they decide to create a business of their own. They're the ultimate 'slashies'. 'Slashie' is an unfairly pejorative term used by those who want to criticise millennials for their complex LinkedIn profiles. A slashie might be an accountant who is also a photographer, milliner and weekend city tour operator. The old economy rewarded employees for their steadfast service, spending 35 years of their life with a company in a static role before being rewarded with a wristwatch and a handshake at retirement. Moving jobs regularly was the sign of an employee who was unreliable, uncommitted or dodgy. Today, it's rare for employees to spend more than three or four years in a role – in fact, being tenured in one role for a decade is sometimes (incorrectly!) considered to reflect an individual's lack of ambition.

Do you think you're a slashie? If so, you're in good company! I myself am a writer, director of a digital strategy agency, blogger, podcaster, Head Girl of Serious Women's Business: Northside and freelance journalist. In order to flourish professionally, we all need our skillsets to have dimensionality – thus our ever-expanding list of 'can-dos'. Here's the rub, slashie: you're likely used to touting your long list of skills at networking events, Facebook Groups, coworking spaces, gyms and baby showers. When someone asks what you do, a burble of half-finished sentences pours from your mouth, drowning your audience in seemingly incoherent chatter. They hear something about 'coaching, life design and influence-making'. They don't have a clue what you do, because at its core you haven't decided yet. If you can relate to this, don't feel bad: it can take a long time to clarify your offering into a perfect elevator speech.

Here's mine: 'I am Director of Ruby Assembly. We provide fully outsourced social media for professional services'.

Here's what mine used to be: 'I'm a commercial copywriter, specialising in real estate and property content. I'm also a blogger and photographer with a focus on arts and culture and a popular real estate blog. I also do social media for a variety of businesses, in addition to live event coverage and dialogue training for women in sales roles. And I've just written a novel.'

Erm, what?

It's not that any of the above is untrue. I do all these things. But when someone asks you what you do – personally or professionally – they're not after your full CV, or some kind of personal checklist of career possibilities. You need to hang your hat on one core idea when you are building your business. Clarity is memorable and powerful. It took me years to pare back my CV-vomit into its current, concise form. In my case – and in the case of entrepreneurs I've mentored and entrepreneurs like yourself – the paring back feels painful. It feels like you're somehow cheating yourself out of a job opportunity, or pigeonholing yourself into one immovable role if you don't trot out every aspect of your offering.

I understand this reticence completely. I remember how difficult it was to stop including the word 'blogger' in my elevator speech. I wanted people to know that I had an opinion, that I was wanted in social circles and that I had a popular following. That's the blogger or influencer's currency – their demand, their audience. I was attached to the little moniker. But after much introspection, I realised that being an influencer wasn't actually at the core of my business. In fact, it earned me very little revenue compared to my key offering of fully outsourced social media. Of course, I continue to blog, and now I focus on podcasting too. Just because it's not in my elevator speech doesn't mean all my slashie skillsets have ceased to be. My business offers copywriting, blog content, event coverage, photography, videography, newsletters, ebooks and social media content – but it's the social media content I need my audience to know about first and associate me with. From there, all the other offerings naturally flow.

This book outlines a very practical course. It asks you to work with the strengths and skills you have today, rather than being an exercise in possibility. I want you to identify one powerful thing or service you can sell right now. Not all the things – just one thing. As you'll soon come to see, specificity and clarity send a strong message to the marketplace. By narrowing your initial offering to one or two key items, you'll be able to express what you do with ease (avoiding years of slashie ego-driven elevator speech vomits). For example, 'Hi, I'm Giulia. I help small businesses with their tax compliance', or, 'Hi, I'm Jane. I make beautiful wedding cakes'. Simple, right? Right! Such clarity does take work to arrive at, however, which is where this week's activities come to the fore.

BRAVE ACTIVITY: Going clear

Set aside two hours to define and simplify your potential business offering. You don't need to set whatever you arrive at in concrete, but the clarification process will strengthen your business offering and prevent you from saying 'yes' to everything and everyone who expresses the vaguest interest in your burgeoning business.

Here are some questions to help you dive deeper into your observations; apply them to each of the business concepts you're still experimenting with, and write your answers down in a beautiful notebook, on your computer or in your 100 Days of Brave Playbook:

- **What's the one thing I can sell today in my business?** This is the premier, numero-uno offering. Is that a great coffee? Exit planning services? Garden maintenance for a particular suburb? Name it and claim it.
- **What are the next two things I can sell today in my business?** These are the two ancillary offerings that support your

centrepiece. If your business is selling oracle cards, your ancillary offerings could be selling affirmation cards and giving tarot readings. If your business is family wills, your ancillary offerings could be conveyancing and negotiating pre-nups. Be clear on these.

· **What is an offering I do not want to include in my service?** You might not want to work in other people's businesses. You might not want to provide a layby service. You might not want to work with brands that sell diet products. You probably won't know all the things you won't want to do until someone asks you to do them: take note of your gut feeling in these situations. Do you want to be paid on a 15-day cycle, or would you be content to wait for 30-day or 60-day payments? Although these are terms of trade, they are still part of your business offering.

· **How is my business of greatest service to people?** Identifying this may help reveal the most important offering you can provide.

· **Can I truthfully provide the service or product I am selling?** If not, dump it (for now). 100 Days of Brave is about helping you create an actionable business in three months, not navel-gazing and signing up for a new degree. By all means, learn as you go – but make sure you can genuinely offer your clients the service or product you are selling ASAP.

· **Is this a real business offering or a vanity piece?** You might have a hobby you love, but loving something doesn't make it a viable business offering. Some things are best left as passion projects! Consider your 'saleable' items shrewdly: are these services or products people genuinely want? Will they pay their hard-earned for them? We'll talk about pricing in chapter 13, but for now, consider whether the hourly wage you'll associate with your service is viable – or if it should be a pleasure project for the weekend.

Chapter 8

What's in a name?

Quite a lot, actually

Phew! By this stage, you've done a lot of the foundation work necessary for beginning your business. It's likely that you've now decided upon the business concept you're going to pursue and have tested it as rigorously as you can with vox pops, surveys and brainstorming. Well done! Now it's time to play – get ready to name your business! Intuitively, I'd guess you know that business names are important. You may already have one in mind, or you might be completely stumped. This week is all about using creative means to formulate a business name to build your new life upon.

When I named Ruby Assembly (or as it was known back then, Ruby Slipper), it was like a bolt from the heavens. I knew that I was on the cusp of beginning a copywriting business and that my clients were probably going to come from the real estate and property industries. I was sitting on the couch watching *The Wizard of Oz* when I saw those magical, glittering slippers on the screen and heard Dorothy Gale repeat her mantra 'There's no place like home' three times. BAM. Ruby Slipper was the perfect name for my business: it matched my penchant for whimsy, it encapsulated the sense of magic I bring to my work, and it had subtle ties to the idea of home and property. It was like manna from heaven, that name. It also gave me the possibility to grow with my business as it scaled, and it didn't restrict my activities as a business. Imagine if I'd chosen to name my business 'Iolanthe's Real Estate Copywriting', or 'Property Writers'. I could have poured years of effort and resources into a business name that defined me into a corner! I could have spent thousands on websites and branding before realising I wanted to do more than just real-estate-centric content.

A word to the wise: business names that are not directly related to the function of your enterprise are powerful. They're nimble, as they allow you to scale and grow as you develop your specialty as a business owner. You might start out working in one niche (say, contract law, or children's clothing) before expanding into another market (for example, family law, or shoes). What's more, businesses with names unrelated to their function statistically sell for more.

Additionally, creating a name without an obvious meaning or provenance gives your customer the space to have their interest piqued and to engage with your business's story. In a world in which generic brands are becoming ubiquitous, the small (or seemingly small) business with a true story that connects is very much in demand. Large brands use the same principles to give a sense of intrigue and legitimacy to their business. Victoria's Secret (who's Victoria again, and what is that bird hiding?), Bondi Sands (it's Australian, but what does it sell?) and The Beach People (they sound like my people, let me join the club!) are all excellent examples of big businesses using names as vehicles for their products. Whether Victoria's Secret evolves into a beauty company, Bondi Sands chooses to create a bikini each summer in addition to their tanning products, or The Beach People move from 'roundie' towels to blow-up pool toys, their names don't niche them into one offering alone.

While you're doing the important work of developing a name for your business, also consider developing a by-line and a hashtag.

Let's look at the role that each of these plays in conjunction with your business name.

By-lines

A by-line serves to reinforce a business name. This is particularly valuable for business names that are personal or unconnected to their service offering. By-lines can be positioning statements that communicate the values of a business, or they can explain a business's offering or product. By-lines are sometimes part of a logo, or used in addition to a logo where appropriate. Here are a few well-known examples of by-lines, for reference:

- **Just Do It:** Nike's by-line is a positioning statement that is a general catch-all about being determined and having forward momentum. It's related to sport, but it goes beyond that to be more generally a positive aphorism about life. 'Nike' itself is a name that means little to those unfamiliar with Greek mythology, so the Just Do It by-line has to do much of the heavy lifting about the company's purpose.
- **Down down, prices are down:** Replete with a jingle Australians have heard more times than they'd care to remember, this successful by-line for supermarket Coles encapsulates their core offering to the consumer: they're the cheapest, and they offer great value. This by-line is repeated across their branding, differentiating Coles from their competitors through sheer hypnotism! Like it or loathe it, we collectively understand the message when we see the big pointy red finger and hear 'down down, prices are down'.
- **I'm lovin' it:** McDonald's began their slow transformation from burger joint with a scary clown mascot to casual family

restaurant and café by hiring Justin Timberlake to perform a tune around their new-look by-line: 'I'm lovin' it'. With a positioning statement that's purely about pleasure and how tasty their offering is, McDonald's have since expanded into more adult markets by broadening their offering into McCafés and providing healthier options such as wraps. 'I'm lovin' it' engages with the core emotion we want to feel around food, bypassing entirely conversations around health and wellness while simultaneously evoking both.

Unlike a business name, by-lines can be changed and developed as the brand grows, so they provide the opportunity to enjoy a little experimentation. Once upon a time, Coles's by-line was 'New World' (yes, I too am confused by this). The by-line of Australian department store Myer used to be 'My Store Myer'. Point being, don't get too hung up on perfecting your by-line first up. You may choose not to have a by-line at all! The process of attempting to develop one, however, can help you to focus with greater attention on your core business offering or value – a useful exercise of its own.

When Ruby Slipper (as it was known then) was born, my initial by-line was 'There's No Place Like Home'. At the time, it made perfect sense: it tied in with *The Wizard of Oz* provenance and connected with my initial client base, which was the property industry. This by-line is emblazoned on my first set of cutesy-pie business cards, featuring a sugar-almond pair of red slippers. As months and years wore on, however, I realised that I never really used this by-line. That was partially because I felt it was a bit too twee, and also because Ruby Slipper quickly branched out into serving a wide variety of businesses. For years, I had no by-line for my business – until I was undertaking the process of designing a set of seasonal posters advertising Ruby Slipper, which were to be pasted up around inner Melbourne on hoardings. Like a bolt from the blue, my perfect by-line AND hashtag came to me: '#MoreThanLikes'. I'm so proud of this by-line, as it encapsulates the values of my business (namely, that social media and communications are a much deeper project than simply the 'likes' on the surface of a Facebook page) and the fact that we do more than simply social media. There's no way I could have come up with this by-line if I had been focused squarely on doing so: instead, it percolated in my brain until it was ready to rise the surface as a fully formed concept. Just magic… that took eight years to eventuate.

Hashtags

Hashtags are related to by-lines. Your hashtag might be interchangeable with your by-line, or it might not be. A product of the digital era, hashtags serve three key purposes:

1. **Branding:** Like a by-line, a hashtag reiterates your brand. It is also an implied invitation for customers to tag you in their posts.
2. **Searchability/Geolocation:** Initially, a hashtag's key purpose was to make your content searchable. Adding a hashtag to your Instagram, Facebook or Twitter post meant that others would be able to find your content with ease. Such hashtags could be based on your location (such as #Melbourne), a genre (such as #Blogger) or an event (such as #MelbourneWritersFestival).
3. **Humour and context:** Arguably the most important aspect of a hashtag is to inject humour and add necessary context to images. Whether making a dubious meme less politically incorrect, aligning your business to a cause (for example, '#YES'), or referring to pop-culture ('#KeepingUpWithThe'), hashtags serve as a wink to your audience.

*

You will likely develop firmer ideas around your by-lines and hashtags as you work on your business during the next trimester. For now, know that by-lines and hashtags are part of the naming process, and take note of any good ideas for either that pop into your consciousness.

Paralysis by analysis

Before you begin the exciting process of creating a name, by-line and hashtag for your business, a word of warning inspired by J.R.R. Tolkien's Gandalf: 'Keep it secret, keep it safe'. Naming your business is an intimate process that should be a private affair. This is not a time to post your proposed business names on LinkedIn or Facebook to have random strangers offer their critiques.

I scream a little on the inside when I see people posting their nascent logos or business names into the ether, exposing their precious babies to the ravages of the internet before they've even sprouted them into a fleshy business concept. The great unwashed (bless 'em!) haven't done the research you've done about your business category and concept. They might not be your audience. Asking your whole LinkedIn or Facebook audience their opinion on something like a name (which should be well considered) also makes you look amateurish. On top of this, there's also IP (intellectual property) to take into account – don't go sharing your potential name with the world before you've registered it, because some cheeky monkey (or vast multinational) could take it. As this chapter illustrates, the name of a business represents the culmination of so much hard work – you don't want to throw all that work away.

At this fragile time, random opinions given by punters without context are not valuable to your project. And opinions are like assholes – everyone's got one. Depending on your temperament, it can be hard to make a decision on a name for your business; don't make this decision more complex by paying attention to others' opinions, as this will protract the process and confuse you further.

In closing – be brave! One of the great pleasures – and challenges – of being a business owner is being a sole decision-maker. Become comfortable with backing yourself, and go forward with confidence.

BRAVE ACTIVITY: The name game

Set aside four hours to brainstorm and decide upon a name, by-line and hashtag for your business. There's no 'right' way to do this, and I recommend a variety of techniques to assist the naming Muse in her work. It's possible that you won't settle upon a name during this time: what you're doing is opening your subconscious to suggestion. To get woo-woo about it, you're setting the intention of finding a name for your business. Delivery will be shortly forthcoming, so fret not.

In manageable blocks of half an hour or so per day, engage with your intuition in the best way you know how. This could be by meditating, binging Netflix, reading, journalling, vision-boarding or using divination tools. Note every name, by-line and hashtag that arises meaningfully in a beautiful notebook, on your computer or in your 100 Days of Brave Playbook. Here are some ideas to get the creative juices flowing:

· **Consider your own name:** Twinings. Harvey Norman. Using part of your name – or even a nickname – can be a great branding tactic. It brings your story and your own personal brand into direct contact with your audience, which is powerfully beneficial. Customers love a story of provenance!

- **Reflect on your heroes:** Ernest Hemingway. Oprah Winfrey. Your granny Delilah. Are there any individuals you admire who have names that could work for your business? Think beyond the name of the hero, too: what were the foods, places, colours or ideas these individuals were drawn to? Take note of any words that really grab your attention.
- **Places of meaning:** Cast your mind back to places where turning points in your life story occurred. You might think of a grand adventure to Portugal. You might think of your primary school playground. Are there any words here that might match your business?
- **Tall tales:** Whether you're a bookworm, a movie buff or a Netflix binger, think of stories that have really struck a chord with you. You never know... you might just find your very own Ruby Assembly in the mix!

Chapter 9

Taxing matters

Set your business up for compliance success

If there's one thing you must achieve during Brave Beginnings, it is setting your business up for success in terms of compliance. I know tax and business registration isn't the most exciting thing to work through, but if you do it right first time around, you give your business the best chance of success and the capacity to grow safely (while reducing the likelihood of getting into debt to the taxman).

Take a moment and consider: how does this call to action about tax compliance make you feel?

Some would-be entrepreneurs I've mentored have remarked that they'll invest time into setting up their business structure 'when they've started making money'. It's almost as though they doubt their business concern is going to be a success – which isn't a great platform to begin from. So, I ask you to tackle this step as though your business were already a success. For some of you, this might be difficult, but I ask you to persist – not only will it make the process of compliance more enjoyable, it will compel you to think in greater detail about the kind of business you will run.

I am naturally hypercompliant. I suppose that balances out my appetite for risk when it comes to being an entrepreneur! I wanted to ensure that Ruby Assembly would never leave me in debt to the taxman: everything was going to be above board. And reader, even with the best intent in the world, I still had an episode of debt to negotiate my way through. Despite my desire to be hypercompliant, I was still a newbie to the world of business. I made poor decisions that many small-business owners make as they ramble their way through the world of startup and scaling.

The first point I'd like to make is: most small-business owners have to deal with a debt to the taxman at some point. And it's not because they're negligent or ill-meaning: it's usually because they've had poor quality tax advice (or no tax advice at all). With the help of the 100 Days of Brave process, you may be able to avoid this circumstance. But if you do encounter it, know that you're totally normal and not some kind of blackguard criminal on the run from the law. This too will pass.

When I began Ruby Assembly, I knew that I should register my business and acquire an ABN (Australian Business Number). I hopped onto the website and registered, wearing my hypercompliant hat. I thought that registering for GST (goods and services tax) would make me additionally compliant and less likely to run into tax troubles, and so I went ahead and did so. I also availed myself of the small-business education seminars run by the Australian Taxation Office (ATO), attending three or four in the first few months of being in business. While valuable, these seminars had a real edge of scaremongering about them: they were effectively '101 Ways to Get into Tax Debt' sessions. For those in startup who were a bit laissez-faire about compliance, this message was undoubtedly useful and encouraged people to take actions. In my case, it only heightened my concern about the million and one ways I could fall into debt, making me even more certain about my decision to register my fledgling business for GST. This was my first big compliance mistake.

I already had an accountant who I'd used for several years, with whom I lodged my annual tax return when I worked in real estate. I trusted him and had worked with him from the age of 21 – he had a successful business and I chose to continue using his services when I began Ruby Assembly. After all, he'd been able to recoup a neat few-thousand tax return for me year-on-year. Not understanding the critical role of an accountant during the startup of a business was at the heart my second big compliance mistake.

As I want to help you avoid compliance mistakes and being in debt to The Man, I'll share my startup stuff-ups with you. Goodwill and ignorance about the taxation system is not enough to help you grow your business or escape the taxman's tithe (as my experience with the ATO quickly taught me). Both of my mistakes were born of attempting to do the right thing – which is why it's so important to really focus on compliance, as it's not intuitive. Know too that most small-business owners end up in a conundrum similar to my own; it's the result of a business growing and doing well! So, if you get there, know that it's a rite of passage, and will be overcome with some negotiation and good counsel from an accountant.

My GST mistake

Being hypervigilant about GST and wanting to avoid being in debt to the tax department left me with a tax debt. Three things led me to choose to register my business for GST: the first was the ATO seminars, which consolidated my fear of tax debt. The second was a misguided belief that having GST included in my fee made me appear more professional to clients. The third was the assumption that registering for GST wouldn't have that big of an impact on my finances.

Fact: in Australia, you only need to register for GST if you expect to earn $75,000 or more per year. Reader, I did not make $75,000 in my first year. I did not have to register for GST, and being a compliance pollyanna cost me. When you first begin in your startup, you may not charge the full whack you're worth. I hope you do, but I didn't: I was selling content and wasn't aware of my own value, or the value of the products I made. I was building GST into these already inexpensive quotes, which meant I was stealing from myself with every invoice. The ATO didn't care that I earned under $75,000 when it came to the end of the financial year – I had registered and charged clients for GST, and I owed them those dollars regardless. These repayments were hefty against my low income and affected my quality of life.

Please consult with an accountant before making the decision to register your business for GST – unless you truly have to, avoid doing so until necessary.

My accounting mistake

Like many newbie entrepreneurs, I attempted to do as much of my own bookkeeping as possible. I must admit that this did benefit me, as it bettered my understanding of quarterly business activity statements (BAS) and GST document submission. But in other ways, it disadvantaged me and made accurately charting my business growth and projected income very difficult. I was sending invoices using Word documents (without invoice numbers – always use invoice numbers!), using Excel spreadsheets to record my monthly expenditure and a notepad to jot down amounts clients owed me. It was very lo-fi. I also kept to my routine of visiting the accountant annually for my tax return submission.

Let me tell you: there are accountants, and there are accountants. Your average garden-variety accountant will help you with basic compliance, such as helping you lodge your individual tax return annually. You don't want one of these people; what you want is an accountant who looks beyond compliance and is able to offer you strategic advice that not only minimises tax, but prevents you from getting into pickles with the ATO and other regulatory bodies.

When I first began Ruby Assembly, I had a compliance-based accountant. He was a nice enough fella who I already had a business relationship with. However, he wasn't a strategic accountant who actively sought to improve my position as a business or protect my assets as an individual. Upon reflection, he certainly wasn't an ideal match for me, an entrepreneur in startup. He assumed that I knew more than I did about tax obligations, and gave me lodgement that was a terrible mismatch for my startup income (read: very close to nil).

Long story short: after a couple of years in business, Ruby Assembly began to make more money (yay)! Not a load more, but a slow trend of growth had appeared. I dutifully went to my accountant's office with my carefully produced Excel spreadsheets (I wasn't using accounting software at this time, which was also to my detriment). My accountant looked over my numbers and suggested that I should lodge my return at the latest date possible. His logic was that this would give me more time with my saved monies due to the ATO; after all, it's better in my pocket than the taxman's right? Wrong. So very wrong. Not informing the ATO about my growing income was to my disadvantage – I kept on paying my tax for the following year, but I was paying too little. This advice ultimately put me into $10,000 of debt with the ATO. I have chalked it up to experience – but it was the result of my ignorance and my accountant's inability to warn me about the risks of nonreporting. Pro tip: pay the taxman monies owed ASAP, and always let them know what you're earning, to avoid my conundrum.

A note on accounting software

Thanks to cloud technology, accessible and intuitive accounting software is readily available to entrepreneurs in startup. My choice is

Xero (not sponsored; just good!) as it fulfils several core needs in my business:

- My accountant has back-end access to my books 24-7 to help me if I run into balancing issues.
- I can easily invoice clients and keep track of my accounts payable.
- It takes care of my obligations around weekly payments, tax, holiday and superannuation obligations on behalf of my employees.
- I have a good sense of cashflow, which allows for solid funds management.

There are many cloud-based products that will do a similar job; I recommend getting a basic subscription to an accounting software of your choice and being compliant from day dot.

A note on business structure

The structure you choose for your fledgling business really does matter. To be fair, business structure is too complex and personalised a matter to tackle meaningfully in this tome, so I suggest that you utilise your first session with an accountant to decide on the right structure for you. Popular structures include the following:

- **Sole trader:** This is the simplest and least expensive structure. A sole trader is the only owner in their business, and is legally responsible for all aspects of their practice. They may employ workers, but they cannot employ themselves.
- **Trust:** Used for business and investment purposes, trusts offer personal safeguards to individuals. Trusts are treated as taxpayer entities for the purposes of tax administration, and the trustee is responsible for managing the trust's tax affairs.

- **Company:** Companies have a separate legal existence from their owners, who are known as 'members' or 'shareholders'. Small-business owners often use a company structure called a 'proprietary limited company', which does not sell its shares and has limited liability.

Don't freak out about debts

So, you've got a tax debt. Congratulations, kiddo! That probably means your business is making money! Getting a tax debt is something that happens to most small-business owners: it's a funky rite of passage and is best viewed in that light. When I first realised my debt, I felt deep shame. How could I have got myself into $10,000 of debt? And how in God's name was I going to repay it?

Many other entrepreneurs have shared with me this sense of failure around accruing a tax debt. Please don't freak out if debt happens to you. See it as a signpost from the universe to take things to the next level with your business, shoring up the boat where you might have noticed it has leaks, and engaging the systems and professional support you need to prevent debt becoming a concern again. The ATO will allow you to create a payment plan to pay down your debt in chunks. I found dealing with the ATO a bit challenging myself – if you begin to feel overwhelmed by your interactions with them, please engage an accountant to do so on your behalf. The money is well spent; you'll end up with more favourable payment plans, and a weight will be lifted from your shoulders. Before you know it, that pesky debt will be paid down (and you'll probably have learned some sneaky saving strategies to boot).

BRAVE ACTIVITY: Compliance on-point

Set aside around four to five hours to address as many of the below compliance tasks as possible. If you don't get around to ticking off the full list, make sure you diarise to do so within your second trimester. Want more support and structure? Your 100 Days of Brave Playbook has a checklist with room for taking notes about each compliance task to tick off. The 100 Days of Brave Facebook Group is also your space to quiz fellow Bravers on their compliance progress.

Here are the compliance tasks to address:

- Register your ABN.
- Register your name, and register your trademark.
- Get insurance.
- Choose accounting software.
- Appoint an accountant.
- Protect your assets – secure relevant trademarks and patents, and choose business structure.
- Appoint a lawyer.
- Secure websites – both '.com.au' and '.com', if your business is based in Australia – and social media handles.
- Open a business bank account (not necessary if you're a sole trader, but a good idea anyway).
- Choose a business structure (sole trader, partnership, trust, company – the accountant, advisor or commercial lawyer will help here).

Chapter 10

Don't quit your day job

Money. You need it.

Many people are attracted to running their own business because of the freedom it offers. And it's quite true: living life on your own terms is part of the entrepreneur deal. Right now, your great idea has you dreaming of your new self-determined lifestyle. Everywhere you go – online and in the real world – you're now hearing stories about other entrepreneurs who wake when they want, enjoy an acai bowl, Instagram their Bircher muesli and have two Skype interviews with clients paying for their expertise. It's all exciting, and by Jove, you want it NOW! You've begun fantasising about handing in your letter of resignation and kissing goodbye to the nine-to-five slog.

Hold your horses. Take a breath. Do some downward-facing dog or watch an episode of *Tiger King*. Please don't quit your day job while your business is in startup. Many entrepreneurs or coaches online spruik a kind of balls-to-the-wall 'all in or you're a weakling' attitude towards beginning a business. Time and again, I've observed this approach result in the failure of business concepts that, given a bit more breathing space and time to develop, could have become going concerns.

Don't believe the hype: it's entirely normal to work one (or more!) jobs while your business is in startup. If your paid employment is in direct competition with your startup and you're at risk of disrespecting your employer, by all means resign – but find yourself another form (or forms) of employment outside of your startup. Here's why.

Startup is a marathon, not a sprint

This business life thing requires stamina. Launching a startup can really take it out of you, so you've got to be gentle with yourself – and your business concept. If you put undue pressure on your startup to support you entirely from the get-go, you're not only likely to stress out and burn through savings or rack up credit card debt, you're also likely to stop believing in your business concept. Don't have unreasonable expectations of your business – just keep on keepin' on by working on it when you can. I'd have to say that this period of time when you're juggling your startup and your existing career is the hurdle at which many would-be entrepreneurs stumble. They want to be able to cleanly step from their full-time gig into their new business, with no downtime in between. In reality, such a circumstance is very rare; unless you're going into a shopfront concern or an ecommerce business with financial backing, many new businesses are born by working on the weekend, working early in the morning or after hours, or by negotiating a four-day work week and doing all you can on a Friday.

During the year when I began Ruby Assembly, I worked four jobs. One was a four-days-per-week position as a business development manager (BDM) at a real estate agency; another was a Saturday job as a receptionist at another real estate agency. I also sold lingerie via a party plan model in lounge rooms all over Victoria. After all this was work was complete, I worked on Ruby Assembly: I delivered my social media content and copywriting while prospecting for new clients.

I often share this story about my job-juggling with people in the throes of startup: people who are feeling trapped by their working day and want to escape into entrepreneurship full-time right this very minute, and those who have taken the leap prematurely and are freaking out about their business dream rapidly devolving into a nightmare. I hope it illustrates the necessary normalcy of continuing to nurture multiple forms of income during the first year (or two) of your business. Sometimes the internet and its shiny, happy business gurus lull us into the idea that a business owner needs to look like a lithe, tanned digital nomad running her empire from Cancún, and that anything other than this fantasy vision is simply not living life on your own terms. I call bullshit on that business fantasy, which has driven plenty of wonderful businesses (and entrepreneurs!) into the ground. If only they had been gentler with their business concept – and themselves – and not put so much financial pressure on their startup! With space, time and persistence, their business might have been a success. Not an overnight one, of course, but I'm pretty sure you know overnight successes are also the stuff of myth and Instagram.

Reflecting on Ruby Assembly's startup year of job-juggling, I don't recall this period of time being anything other than exciting and ripe with possibilities. Sure, I was working hard, but I was so focused on the fact that I was actively building a life on my own terms – meeting new people and thinking about fresh ways to share my business with the world – that the hours weren't onerous. I needed the money to pay for my mortgage, my bills, my groceries. No-one else was going to make that money for me. And nobody else was going to make Ruby Assembly a reality.

Many business owners have a story similar to my own: doing their nine-to-five while working on their own startup after hours. It's a sensible and lower-stakes way to embrace business ownership.

Three reasons to keep your day job

Still fantasising about telling your boss where to stick it tomorrow? Here are three reasons why keeping your day job during startup helps you become a better business owner.

You'll be forced to make better decisions

A wonderful benefit of growing your startup while working your day job is enforced pace. Given that you won't be able to spend every working day beavering away on your project (initially), your business's development and growth is likely to be slower. This might feel frustrating, as by this stage your brain is going to be buzzing with ideas! However, being forced by economic realities to take a slower pace means you're going to make more considered decisions about your business. That precious breathing space helps your brain settle, gives you a sense of perspective and allows you to recognise true gold from fool's gold. While you might feel stymied by your day job, its presence during this startup phase is really a blessing, giving you the means to pay your rent and grow into your new life! Your day job will also give you resources to invest into your new business that simply wouldn't be there if you chucked the towel in – think website, photography, accountants, lawyers, coworking spaces... you get the idea!

You'll discover where your passion lies

Your business might sound amazing on paper. Whether it's an outsourced administration brand, a mobile yum cha van or a lighting business, you've done all your vision-boarding and you're sure it's going to be a winner in the market. You start working on your business, enthused, beavering away a couple of nights a week and on a Sunday. The thing is, after a few months, you may not feel the excitement and joy you expected to feel about your business. In fact, your day job could be a relief compared to the little business you've brought to life.

If this happens to be your experience, feel no shame. Sometimes a business concept may be market-sound and making money – but you just don't love it. Living a life on your own terms doesn't mean swapping your career as a discontented employee for a career as a discontented business owner. Keeping your day job is so important during startup, because it allows you to experiment with your new business emotionally. Do you actually like what you're doing? Is the experience growing you or shrinking you? If it's the former – wonderful! Go forth, keep growing, and quit your day job when it is economically viable to do so. If it's the latter – equally wonderful! Shelve the business idea – or, even better, sell it to another person who wants to make it their life. You've learned what it's like to be in business, and you've learned what you like and what you don't. Importantly, you've had income to support you throughout the startup experiment. Well done!

You'll develop minimum viable product and proof of concept

Keeping your day job also gives you the time to work out if your business concept has legs. Whether you're going it alone in startup or aiming to garner investor support, use your first year in business to develop a really concrete minimum viable product.

What's that? It's the market-acceptable prototype of whatever it is that your business sells. If you're making physical items, this could be your ideal t-shirt, kitchen bench or cargo bike. If you're delivering a service, it could be the systems surrounding terrific client briefing sessions and the subsequent delivery of appropriate coaching, or contracts, or copy, or physiotherapy. In short, keeping your day job while beginning your business gives you the breathing space to better define and refine your offering, establishing proof of concept. This is of terrific value to you as a business owner, as you'll have tested your product and gathered market feedback before perfecting your offer – meaning your chances of success when you go full-time are higher, and your financial risk is lowered.

If you decide to go full-time without establishing minimum viable product and proof of concept, you're taking a big risk. You're putting a huge amount of pressure on your fledgling business and yourself, which can often tip a perfectly good business concept over the edge and straight into oblivion.

*

While this chapter in your first trimester has no particular activities associated with it, I hope my experience and advice helps to quieten your urge to quit everything RIGHT THIS VERY MINUTE OH MY GOD I CAN'T TAKE IT ANOTHER SECOND – and to instead take the pressure off your fledgling business, and yourself as an entrepreneur. Slow and steady wins this race.

Chapter 11

Resourcing your business

Interns, contractors and employees

At this stage of 100 Days of Brave, it's highly likely you're simply thinking of buying yourself a job and freeing yourself from the demands of The Man. When I first set out, being self-employed was my main goal, and I wanted a business that relied on nothing and no-one but me and my two little hands. However, it's equally possible that your particular business model will require more practical assistance from others additional to yourself from its earliest days. In this chapter, I'll share my experience of resourcing my business – from sole-trader status to a becoming a company – and offer the pros and cons of different kinds of staffing and support arrangements.

All by myself

As it may be for many of you, wanting to live life on my own terms was at the heart of my decision to become a business owner. I didn't want to have to answer to anybody except my clients, preferring to collaborate with many parties than to have one single 'boss'. I couldn't see beyond wanting to grow Ruby Assembly into a business that would pay my mortgage and keep me in Netflix subscriptions and brunches. Pretty quickly, however, my business's demands outpaced my capacity to be hands-on and delivering every piece of copy, ghostwritten article, ebook and social media post. Before I knew it, I had to find a way to get comfortable resourcing my business with other people's talent.

This was a tough decision for me, as I was so resistant to the idea of anyone other than myself interacting with my clients, and I certainly never wanted to be an employer. The imaginative jump from 'sole trader' to 'director of a company' was a step too far for me: I simply couldn't conceive of ever having the weighty responsibility of other people's tax payments, superannuation and holiday pay resting on my shoulders. All those contracts. All that risk. EUGH. That was for other people and not me. Of course, all that has changed now, and employing others is a natural and essential part of the organism that is Ruby Assembly. But it wasn't always this way. On my journey to employing staff full-time, I have used a mix of interns, contractors and formal employees to resource my business. Here are some practical pros and cons of each category of resource.

Contractors

Using contractors was my first foray into engaging others' talents for Ruby Assembly. It appeared to me the lowest-risk option for my business, as I couldn't guarantee ongoing work with any certainty. I did feel confident that I could offer regular work, but wanted flexibility in who I engaged and when. I understood that all I would need to do was ensure my contractor had an ABN and informed me whether they were registered for GST or not, and come to terms on a daily or hourly rate for their services. I use contractors within Ruby Assembly to this day for casual work, and recommend contractors as a great starting point for stretching your 'boss' legs. Of course, if you're operating your business from Australia, please carefully read the ATO guidelines on using contractors in your business before proceeding.

Pros and cons

Contractor pros:

- You can engage terrific talent for projects without having to commit to their ongoing employment. This might be the only financially viable way to resource your business in startup.
- Using contractors allows you to scale your business up and down depending on demand. You may not have the resources for a graphic designer or photographer to be a full-time part of your team, but you can still sell this expertise as part of your offering to clients. Once they've agreed to your proposal, you can bring contractors on board to complete the project.
- Using contractors gives you a great preliminary experience of being a boss. I learned so much from my time resourcing using contractors – such as the importance of delivering a really accurate brief to contractors prior to their commencing work! This sharpened my skill when taking briefs from clients, too – it was OK for me to have to go back-and-forth with clients refining an outcome, but it was decidedly uncool (and additionally costly) for contractors to do so.
- Cultivating a crew of contractors you regularly use can help you to cover holidays, sick leave and periods of high demand. It might take some time to build up this group of trusted contractors, but once everyone understands your business, they'll be a blessing!
- Using contractors means resourcing your business without the additional stressors of setting aside holiday pay, tax on behalf of employees and superannuation. For many businesses in startup, becoming a formal employer is simply untenable.

- Contractors allow you to bring expert knowledge into your business. Lawyers, accountants, graphic designers, copywriters – they're all part of an expert contractor mix you may choose to draw upon occasionally.

Contractor cons:

- You can't rely on contractors: you're not formally committed to them, and they're not formally committed to you. If you've got a great relationship with a contractor, it's likely they won't disappoint you. But you are not their only priority. So, make sure you give them notice in advance of work you require them to complete.
- You'll need to train your contractors thoroughly before they'll be able to complete your projects to standard. No matter how talented the individual, they'll still need to be aware of how you like things done. This training is costly in time and can be a real drain on resources if you've got lots of contractors coming in and out of your business.

Contracting pro tip: have your contractors sign off on a 'contractor's agreement' created for your business. This protects you as the business owner, puts some basic understandings in place about pilfering your client list, and details your obligations to the contractor and theirs to you.

Interns

Get ready to open a can of worms whenever discussing the ethics of using interns in businesses! Internships have garnered a bad name over the past 15 or so years. I'd say this is primarily because of the legitimate concern around the economic abuse of individuals.

In the USA, internship culture is taken to the extremes, whereby only the wealthiest of individuals – those ably supported by their families – can afford to work unpaid for prestigious publications or institutions for an extended period of time. This is the first key reason. Clearly, this internship culture amplifies a yawning class divide and locks out swathes of the less-monied from the experience necessary to garner paid employment in a variety of categories. In Australia, internship culture can also be abused, with some businesses using interns full-time and unpaid for a full year or more.

Unfortunately, internships often don't offer fairness of exchange. Fairness of exchange is the only ethical way to utilise interns within your business. They cannot be used to simply photocopy all day, or fetch coffees, pack orders or similar. That is not an education: it is the role of a paid PA. Run properly, internships form an essential element of the tertiary experience. Experience within real businesses with actual demands takes students from the theoretical to the practical. It's untrue that students from marketing, PR or media degrees leave their universities workplace-ready. They need to spend time within lively practices that have the time available to train and guide them, making them much closer to workplace-ready and giving them some semblance of understanding of business culture.

For several years in my business, interns were an essential part of our team. Before Ruby Assembly became the more robust business it is today, I had fewer clients and thus more time to truly run valuable internships that represented fair exchange. I would take an intern on for a minimum of six months for a couple of days a week. It would take me at least half this time to teach them our various systems and structures, our software packages and style guides. During this time, they would literally sit next to me – the Director – and have their work finessed and massaged. It was a true exchange of resources: I would give the intern the skills they needed to work within the industry, and in return the intern would give me their time and support.

If you can truly say you are educating an individual and giving them skills that will ably help them into work, running internships may suit your business.

Pros and cons

Intern pros:

- Having an intern within your business is likely to cost you little in funds. If you are bootstrapping and under-resourced, this may be useful to your business.
- Running an internship program is an ideal way to learn about recruitment and candidate selection. It will begin to hone your skills as an employer!
- An enthusiastic intern can bring great energy and commitment to your business, adding energy to your team culture and making small businesses additionally accountable. Having an intern means you can't simply fob off work for the day – you've got to go in and mentor.
- Once an intern is trained, they will hopefully be able to contribute meaningfully to your business for the period of time they are with you.
- An intern may even become a contractor or an employee!

Intern cons:

- Interns cannot always be relied upon. As you are not a source of income for them, it is possible that you will train an intern for a couple of months before they simply disappear into thin air. This has happened to me before, and it's a big cost in time and energy.
- Training an intern is a big undertaking: you are completing their education and you'll be constantly peppered with questions by them. You'll need to heavily edit or amend their work for much of the time. This is part of the deal on your end, so be ready to teach!

Intern pro tip: you know the saying 'Never work with family or children'? Add friends to this mix when you're recruiting for an intern. While those nearest and dearest to you may want to intern with your business, I recommend recruiting an individual who views you predominantly as their mentor and not as their friend or relative. This benefits you as an entrepreneur (as you're growing into your role as a leader), and it means firmer boundaries and better expectations between intern and mentor.

While I no longer have the time within my business to dedicate hours each week to training interns, I did enjoy the period of time Ruby Assembly offered such programs. It taught me about being an employer and a mentor, it helped me to streamline and refine internal business systems, and it gave me a primer in recruitment – and I made some wonderful friends along the way. I'm proud to say that most of my interns have gone on to work within the industry – which is testament to our contribution to their workplace experience and learning!

Employees

As I mentioned earlier in this chapter, I was initially extremely resistant to using employees in my business. In my mind's eye, I made becoming an employer a bogeyman – towering over me with paperwork, contracts and obligations I felt would stymie me. The reality is that once you're in a position to offer ongoing work with confidence – one clue that you're on your way is when you're regularly using contractors every week and figure you can't run your business without their input – becoming an employer doesn't put that much more responsibility onto the entrepreneur's plate.

In any case, it's not until you have employees that your business will really take off in terms of scale. Employing another person full-time is the ultimate vote of confidence in oneself. Energetically, it's a big signpost to the universe that YOU MEAN BUSINESS. In terms of resourcing your business, employing others full-time is my recommendation (once it's tenable, of course). There's something that happens when you commit to employing another person – the formal, contracted nature of this relationship means that they are dedicated to you. Unlike interns and contractors, employees prioritise your work and can be relied upon day in, day out.

Pros and cons

Employee pros:

- They're in it for the long haul! (At least, that's the idea.) You can rely on your employee being in for their contracted hours and can commit to work for your clients or your business appropriately.
- You're likely to experience a higher level of emotional commitment from employees than you might from a contractor. They're on the business journey with you, and they will be more likely to provide emotional succour and good ideas!
- You can grow your business with employees, and scale more effectively by giving employees client-fronting roles and responsibility. Until you have reliable employees, you're effectively in your business on your ownsome. That's OK for a while, but in the long run it's a lonely and tiring road.
- You can have a holiday! Once your employee is well-versed in your business, you can take a much-needed rest while they hold down the fort.

Employee cons:

- Once employees pass their probationary period and you find they are no longer a good fit for your business, you will need to give them multiple warnings before you give them notice. This is an emotionally tricky process that is best handled with the expertise and advice of a lawyer behind you. When you use contractors, your working relationship is on a casual, ad-hoc basis.

- You'll need to become a manager. This means thinking about your employees' well-being, workloads and areas of potential improvement. This isn't necessarily a con, but some people are not natural managers, and they choose to avoid frank conversations at all costs.
- You'll need to pay superannuation and collect tax on behalf of your employees, which means additional accounting work. Again, this isn't overly complex once you're in the swing of things, but you'll need to collaborate with an accountant to ensure you are compliant.

BRAVE ACTIVITY: Snog, marry... hire?

Spend an hour or so working out what support you will need to run your business. It might be that you will function terrifically in startup on your own. Perhaps you'll need to engage an expert contractor to help you with hours 'on the shop floor', regular graphic design work or administration. Maybe your business model will allow for an internship program.

Refer to your 100 Days of Brave Playbook for a handy worksheet helping you to define how best to resource your business. Whichever way you go, I recommend you engage the services of a contract lawyer to create a simple and effective employment contract for any employee you bring into your business.

Chapter 12

The Two C's

Contracts and copyright

No, I'm not talking about the Chanel motif. It's time to focus on the two critical C's upon which your business foundation relies: contracts and copyright. I know that you might not want to focus on these aspects of entrepreneurship, particularly when you're in startup and might not even consider yourself to have a proper business yet.

In my years of mentoring women in business, I note time and again that they're amazing and inspiring when it comes to coming up with ripper concepts. They're quick to share their knowledge and time. They swiftly get their show on the road and are big on vision-boarding and customer care. What they're not so good at is tackling some of the less creative, 'hard' business aspects of commerce, such as contracts and copyright protection. I have also observed a similar phenomenon when engaging with women looking to invest in real estate or become financially independent. Too many women put financial literacy in the 'too hard' basket, much to their detriment.

So, while you might not act swiftly on the recommendations presented in this, your Brave Beginning, don't wait too long to take care of matters relating to contracts and copyright.

The importance of contracts

Like many business owners in startup, when it came to client agreements in my business I was flying by the seat of my pants. I figured that, being an upstanding, well-meaning individual, I couldn't possibly run into any problems with my clients. Not of any serious legal nature, in any case. This led me to write my own services agreement (a well-written but legally valueless one-page Word document that was essentially useless and offered neither me nor my clients any real security). I didn't even have the nous to copy a generic contract agreement off Google, such was my faith in goodwill.

While I am happy to say I haven't had any truly terrible legal skirmishes, I have had enough bruising and slightly frightening experiences to have now implemented formal services agreements across my business. I contacted both an employment lawyer and an intellectual property lawyer, and put down the dollars to protect my business with comprehensive contracts. Here's why you should prioritise having contracts created for your business.

They are your insurance policy

Contracts for your business are like your healthcare insurance. You don't buy insurances or contracts for when things are going swimmingly – no siree. You buy them for when caca hits the fan. We all assume that everything will run like tickety-boo clockwork in our businesses. And if you're doing a good job, that's hopefully going to be the status quo for most of the time. However, a time will come when a disagreement arises between a client or yourself, or an employee takes issue with your practices. A customer might want to sue you over a product that didn't meet their expectations. You can't avoid these vagaries of business – they're just part of the deal when you're putting yourself out there as an independent entrepreneur. When you're in the throes of client- or customer-induced drama, remember all those times you could go for a massage at 11 a.m. on a Wednesday because you are your own boss. Those four-day weekends working on wi-fi from a hotel by the beach: that's the trade-off for the risk of being in business, peeps.

So, once you come to terms with the idea that something legally dicey will occur in the course of entrepreneurship, you will better appreciate the role that contracts play in your security. They're truly a form of insurance, and they'll protect you when times become tricky. Be warned: they will only protect you if they have been created specifically for you. This is no time to be resorting to Google as your ad-hoc legal counsel. (More on that over the page.)

They make client and supplier management easier

Many potentially great business partnerships or commercial relationships come to messy, ugly culminations as the result of mismatched expectations. Agreements made casually over coffee can be easily (or conveniently) forgotten – and before you know it, you're in an emotional dispute over responsibilities within a business, undertakings made by suppliers or promises made to collaborative partners or employees. Clearly defined roles and expectations mean better business relationships, and a more concrete call to accountability if those relationships begins to fail. Whether you sell kombucha or accounting services, client and supplier management is improved by clear contracting.

They clarify your employer–employee relationship

When you and your employee(s) are getting along like a house on fire, everything's tickety-boo. If you're running a business in startup, the level of interaction you'll have with your team is likely to be very high, and personal relationships and friendships will go on to develop very swiftly. Whether you want more formal boss–employer relationships with your team or (like me) you want an all-in, friends-slash-colleagues life collage in your business, contracts will help keep things chugging along in the right direction.

A formal employment contract should be used for the engagement of employees, contractors and interns. This doesn't mean that you must fork out for a new contract every time you recruit – you'll be able to have a savvy lawyer create these assets to be easily used time and again within your business. Remember, you don't invest in contracts for when everything is ace: they're your insurance policy for when things go skewiff. Both you and your employees will be able to avoid constantly renegotiating your relationship courtesy of a contract, with expectations and responsibilities clearly defined. A great contract will also make you a more appealing employer, as employees want to see their benefits clearly laid out in black and white. You'd be surprised how few small businesses actually use proper employment contracts!

Contracting pro tip: don't make Google your lawyer

By now, I've hopefully sold you on the value of contracts and the multitude of benefits they offer you as a business in startup. It's quite possible that you may be cash-strapped at the moment and can think of a bazillion things you'd rather sink funds into than contracts. This might lead you to Google to look for generic contracts to rip off and amend yourself. Please don't do this – not only because of the sticky little matter of copyright (which I'll get to shortly), but because you simply won't know what their contents are, or how relevant they are to your industry and jurisdiction. Just because a document looks like a contract, it doesn't mean it actually is a contract.

Only recently I was asked to sign a contract by a prospective client – a medium-sized business of some repute. I had a cursory look over the document and felt uncomfortable with some aspects of it, and naturally referred it to my own lawyer before signing. My lawyer then identified various faults with the contract, including the fact that it featured parts of a now out-of-date Victorian health act. Why would this seemingly professional business have copied and pasted contracts that included irrelevant terms from a health act? I was confused and gave the prospective client my lawyer's feedback on the matter. They were somewhat embarrassed by this discovery. In short, bad contracts can not only prohibit you from forming business relationships, they can also make you appear amateurish and unprofessional.

Another example of the negative impact 'googled' contracts can have on your business success is one I encountered only recently with a talented photographer. I regularly purchase subscriptions to various photography and media archives to use in Ruby Assembly's media. One of our favourite one-man-band businesses recently changed up her subscription offerings, going from a single-cost proposition to a graded subscription that separated individual users from agencies. 'Good on her', I thought! It was great to see her thinking about the different clients she had garnered, and I was happy to note she was creating different packages tailored to their use of her media. There were, however, blinding inconsistencies in her offering. So many things were unclear about how we could use her images, and the contract itself was clearly a pastiche. Again, I consulted with my lawyer before proceeding. My lawyer and I developed a simple game plan to question the provider about elements of both her contract and offering, which immediately resulted in her changing aspects of the contract and service.

Despite the photographer being super-talented and a wonderful creative, she hadn't really thought about her business as a business. Like many peeps running startups, she wanted to save on contracts and had rustled up some amateurish terms on her own. I wanted to use her service and pay her properly for her work, so I persisted at my own cost and got counsel to build a better agreement between the two of us. How many other business owners simply saw the poor quality of the agreement and the contract and put it in the 'too hard, too sloppy' basket? She has now tightened up her subscription offerings and seemingly improved her contracts, but how much business did she lose by not considering the practicality of her offer and the quality of her contracts?

Copyright and your business

The second critical C to understand and respect is copyright. There is likely no greyer area of the law than copyright, but as a startuppy, entrepreneurish type, it's important that you understand the key machinations of it, and that you respect it.

Respecting others

I'm a highly educated, well-meaning and intelligent businesswoman, but even I have come a cropper in relation to copyright. And it's not because I was wilfully ignoring others' copyright – rather, I was lulled into a false sense of security paired with a serious copyright blind spot (no doubt influenced by observing lax industry practice and social media sharing norms). So, learn from my mistakes, and be sure to only ever use media that you have explicit permission to use, or that you have paid for permission to use.

Here are some of the most common examples of copyright infringement. You'll see them all the time, and you may even be surprised by a few:

- Uploading images from the internet onto Facebook that you do not have explicit permission to use. Yes folks, Facebook, Instagram, Twitter and LinkedIn – not to mention blogs and the internet more generally – seem purpose-built to help you infringe copyright! Individuals and businesses infringe copyright constantly, but that's no excuse when it comes to a court of law. Every time you upload a picture of your favourite royal, or artwork from the Louvre, you are infringing copyright.

· RG (or regramming) images on Instagram. Whether you're using an app or acknowledging the source you've copied the image from (for example, RG @rubyassembly), regramming remains copyright infringement if you have not individually been given permission to share the image.

· Using popular music or film to add flair to your YouTube vlogs. Be very sure of your copyright when it comes to creating video. Haven't paid for it or subscribed to a service that gives you use of it? Best you make up your own theme song, then.

Right now, you're probably 'but'-ing all over the place: 'But (insert shoe brand here) always uses images of this celebrity!'; 'But my mate Kylie at (insert PR business here) has been curating her business's Instagram feed entirely from RGs for years, so that must be OK, right?'

Wrong. So very wrong. We've collectively been lulled into a sense of entitlement and ignorance by social media's speed of easy media sharing, and old wives' tales of nobody being brought to task for infringing copyright. The reality is that copyright owners do uphold their rights – be they photographers, filmmakers, designers or writers – and that if you use their media without permission or purchase, you can be sued. It's a thing. Don't play Russian roulette with your business in startup by exposing your hard work and brilliant ideas to the risk of copyright infringement. (I'll provide you with handy ways to safely use a variety of beautiful media in your second trimester, never worry.) I know it seems super-convenient to build your brand or develop an achingly gorgeous Instagram feed by simply plagiarising others, but the cost of copyright infringement is too high to bear thinking about.

Enforcing your own

Whether you're a writer, an artist, a technologist or an industrial designer, you have copyright over your creative works. You have the right to enforce this copyright, and to protect your intellectual property from being stolen and reused for profit by others. This is yet another reason why engaging with a lawyer for a startup 'once-over' is so important! Educating yourself about your intellectual property rights, and even trademarking logos or concepts, can add terrific value to your business should you sell it in future.

At this early stage of your business, you might not realise the full commercial potential of your idea or product. You may be subconsciously second-guessing the sheer brilliance of your concept. But if you don't take some basic steps (now, or in the near-ish future) to safeguard your intellectual property, you could see hundreds of replicas of your beautiful t-shirt design, or rip-offs of your healing event, plastered all over the internet. I recommend an introductory consult with an intellectual and copyright lawyer so you at least understand the safeguards you might take around your business in future.

BRAVE ACTIVITY: Lawyer up

Connect with your local business community or go on a Google or Instagram stalk to find an intellectual property and copyright lawyer. You might not have the dosh to spend on them right now, but some lawyers will offer a free first consultation. Others might offer intro events for small-business owners where you'll be able to pick up some handy knowledge.

Chapter 13

Pricing

Charge as much as you possibly can

When it comes to running a business, you will need to make money. Money is a funny old thing. It brings up lots of feels. Attitudes towards money – much like our political persuasions and other core values – are often learned within our families. I grew up in a creative family where big money was considered the preserve of the ultra-rich and the morally ambiguous. Teachers were never paid enough, universities were always short on funding: money was held in the hands of the wrong people. My ideas about money have changed over time, and it is likely that as an entrepreneur, your ideas about money will change as well.

Things to consider

I'll often have people ask me, 'How much can I charge for X service?' This is a normal question to ask, but the reality is this:

1. You should charge as much as you possibly can.
2. You must be confident in the price that you present to clients.

So, really, pricing your offering is a bit of a juggling act. Here are a few nuggets around pricing you might consider.

Awards guides are useful... but only up to a point

Many creatives such as writers or designers often quiz me on how much they should charge their clients. There are usually industry awards you can refer to that give general guidelines, which can be considered a starting position. But don't limit yourself to what others are pricing. It's easy to fall into a terrifying vortex of looking at others' pricing and comparing yourself, letting your ego get carried away before deciding that you need to charge less because customers won't pay more for your product than X competitor's. Decide upon a price you're happy to start work at, and go to it.

Negotiation is OK and necessary

I know a super-smart lady who is an expert in her field. She went out on her own as a consultant, but found she wasn't having any luck getting traction with clients. When I asked her why, she'd say that clients simply wouldn't pay enough for her service, and her accountant had told her in no uncertain terms that she had to charge X amount. She was too rigid with her pricing, and her business failed as a result. Think about providing tiered services (or products, or experiences) so that any client can have a bit of your magic in a unitised form. If they're happy with your offering, they'll come back and buy more! Be ready to negotiate or provide solutions that fit their budget.

Quoting is a confidence game

I have a challenge I set with myself: whenever I deliver a new client proposal, I will attempt to charge just a little bit more than my last accepted proposal.

For many years, I did not lift my rates. This was because I was resting on my laurels, and also lacked confidence in my expertise. It can feel difficult to have a conversation with an existing client about price – whether that's for the price of your writing, or the amount you need to charge for a cuppa joe or gardening per hour. But it is a conversation worth having, as it allows you to illustrate value and improve your bottom line.

I was always confident in my work, but stepping into your role as an expert whose years of valuable knowledge are built into your price is where real development lies. Like many small-business owners, I avoided increasing costs to my existing clients because I thought that I might lose their business. How wrong I was! So, I might not have lifted their rates uniformly to match those of my newest clients, but their monthly invoices certainly went up! This in turn gave me the opportunity to grow my business, hire more support, and improve and diversify my offerings. There were no downsides to charging appropriately for my time.

The reason I challenge myself to charge that little bit more each proposal is because I am focused on breaking through my preconceived notions of value. For years, I kept my fees pretty static due to limiting ideas founded on what I understood other people were charging. Really, what other people are charging isn't my business at all. Their work has no bearing on my own. And as I'm ready to negotiate a win-win scenario for every person who comes to my business – except for douchebags who treat waitstaff badly, and those special individuals relentlessly obsessed with return on investment (ROI) – I'm unafraid of people telling me I'm too expensive. That's OK – I'm happy to create a bespoke solution to match their needs that respects both my expertise and their budget as it stands today. Or I can respectfully stay in touch with them and check back in to work with them when they are better resourced.

Pricing your service is all about confidence in communication and testing your own boundaries and assumptions.

Consider value pricing

The legal community in particular is going gaga over the concept of value pricing, as many practitioners move away from itemised invoicing towards offering outcome-based costings for their clients. Value pricing is a great way to practice negotiation for your services, pricing your product based on its value to the customer.

An example would be if someone wants a birthday cake for tomorrow morning that is unicorn-Justin-Bieber-themed. You'll need to stay up all night to complete the project, so it will be costed for your expertise, the time and the inconvenience of short notice. If you had three weeks' notice about the alarming-sounding torte, with ample time to get your ingredients and plot your week's baking, your price wouldn't be quite as exxy.

Another example of value pricing might be found in hairdressing or copywriting: if you have the principal or owner of the business doing your hair or writing your copy, their speed, expertise and capacity to accurately interpret your brief is reflected in the cost of their service. You can amplify your price for inconvenience, rarity, experience and quality – this is a great one to brainstorm over!

The pleasures and perils of collaboration

Collaboration with other parties can lead to problems with pricing and value. On one hand, collaborating with a friend to offer a service can be super! You might be a photographer who chooses to pair up with a framing expert, or a copywriter who pairs up with a graphic designer, for a packaged deal you promote on your website. In theory, such collaborations are terrific – particularly if you both have substantial mailing lists to advertise your joint offer to. But on the other hand, advertising an exclusive collaboration partnership can actually be to your disadvantage.

'How's that?' you ask. Because other businesses who refer their clients to you might sense a conflict of interest. Your other framer may stop referring clients needing photography onto you, or your other graphic design referral partner might send their copywriting clients elsewhere, because you have a formal, advertised relationship with their competitor.

In short, collabs can be excellent – I regularly refer to a variety of amazing complementary businesses in my own practice – but think twice about advertising collaborations as priced packages online. It dissuades other businesses from referring their clients to you, and standardised packages can give potential customers unreasonable expectations around price – for example, they might think your basic package is suitable for their complex project.

Should your prices be on your website?

Oooh, the question of whether to list your prices on your website is a sticky one with no single 'right' answer! If you're a retailer, it makes sense that your prices are clear. This might not be appropriate if you're in the line of bespoke products of *haute joaillerie* and the like, but if your product is ready to wear or use, pricing is essential. Having prices on your products also allows you to use occasional discounting to maximum effect by displaying the normal price and the discount price alongside one another.

If you offer a service, however, having your pricing online can be a disadvantage. Services are, by their very nature, usually a bespoke offering, created to the requirements of the client. Whether you're a florist or an accountant, it's unlikely that your clients' needs will fit into a 'one-size-fits-all' service schedule. Having your prices displayed on your website as a service-based business can limit your capacity to charge appropriately for your offering.

Some clients are easy to service, requiring a reasonable or minimal amount of your time. Other clients can take hours from your day (and years from your life, if you're not careful) for what is ostensibly exactly the same service delivery. It would be grossly unfair for you to charge these clients the same amount as your easier clients, because they are using your service quite differently. By all means, you may choose to have a 'starting at' price list on your website, but hard and fast rules for services can mean tears before bedtime for business owner and customer alike.

It's also nobody's business what you might be charging your clients. Every client relationship in a service-based industry is a negotiation, and your quote for work should be in response to their brief. This is pretty hard to standardise, which is another reason to avoid having your prices on your website, service provider.

Lastly, if you present prices as standardised and upfront, there are two groups of people who will be looking at these figures: your competition and price-driven clients. While it is entirely possible to convert price-driven clients to understanding your value, giving them your costs upfront without asking anything of them isn't helpful to your cause. It's better for them to interact with you before receiving a quote, giving you more control of the client relationship from the get-go. Also, it's handy to know who needs your help! If you list your prices on your website, some potential clients may consider your services and ultimately decide against proceeding without you ever knowing; by requiring them to contact you to obtain pricing information, they have to make you aware of them while they are still considering working with you, giving you the opportunity to win them over.

If you do choose to display your pricing on your website, make your prospective clients earn it! Ensure they fill out a pop-up form that asks for basic details, including their email address and some information on the kind of project they're looking to have fulfilled. Data is valuable, and it's only fair that your exchange of sensitive pricing information is rewarded with the capacity for you to follow up with the potential client!

Common mistakes made when pricing

Here are some 'don'ts' to avoid as often as possible.

Don't charge less because you perceive yourself to be inexperienced or junior

It's nobody's business whether you've been a plasterer for five decades or five weeks. If you are taking money from someone for doing a job, it means that you can do the job. (If you can't do the job, don't take money until you're confident you truly can deliver on your promises – but I bet you can do it, you little champ.)

Be very cautious about accepting payment in 'exposure'

As a commercial blogger, I have been in the invidious position of pitching a full campaign of content, only to be offered payment in event tickets and parking. I was incensed by this, but it's partially my own fault for not setting expectations with the brand upfront. Still, know that many organisations – particularly magazines and other publications, PR brands, and events companies – may try pay you in 'exposure'. Ain't nobody's electricity bills being paid for in exposure, baby. Or their handbags, for that matter.

That said, there are occasions when exposure or payment in kind can be valuable – but weigh up effort versus reward. If you're putting in X hours' work, or providing an item that is worth X amount of dollars, make sure any return on investment balances for you.

'Handshake' agreements, or assignments without briefs

No, I'm not talking about working sans undies in the lounge room (trust me, we've all been there, #amirite)! I'm talking about taking on work that isn't formally quoted and agreed upon, that has no clear scope (or brief). This is more relevant for service-based businesses than retailers – but retailers can still fall foul of handshake agreements with their own suppliers, so be cautious! It's easy to have a terrific meeting with a client and, with the good vibes flowing, you commit yourself to working with them. This fortuitous start can quickly lead to heartache and angst when you and your client have entirely different expectations. They may expect 45,000 revisions of their work for the price of your first draft. Their turnaround times may not match your timeframe. They might experience bill shock, and you could end up chasing an invoice for 18 months. Talk about a downer.

Such loose-ended working arrangements are a lose-lose for everyone involved. My recommendation is to keep those good initial meeting vibes flowing, but create a services agreement detailing your offering and quote, response to their brief, and payment terms. Don't forget to add costing for additional time (editing, meetings, and so on). You may want to consult your friendly local lawyer for this, which is money very well spent. Once the client has taken a breath, read the document and signed off, you can proceed to collaborate with them in much more comfort.

In closing, here are a couple of things to mull over when developing your price structure in this week's activity:

- Unlike employees, entrepreneurs don't have holiday pay, superannuation or sick leave. Be mindful of this when pricing your service or product.

- You are an expert, or you are producing a product or delivering a service that took inspiration, dedication, education and a significant investment of time to create. This expertise has a value – otherwise people would make the item you're selling or do the task you're completing themselves.

BRAVE ACTIVITY: More money, fewer problems

Spend around two hours pricing your offering or product for the market. Look to awards as a foundation, then think about a fair hourly rate for your expertise. You might want to jump on industry-relevant forums and ask how members of your community price their services. Don't diminish your value or 'race to the bottom' with pricing – your relative newness to business doesn't make you inexpert or junior.

Refer to your 100 Days of Brave Playbook for a handy pricing worksheet, helping you to collate a variety of potential pricings before arriving on a structure that works for now. Stay fluid – and if you provide a service, remember that negotiation is part of the deal. Set a baseline and work upwards from there!

Chapter 14

Tell me about your business

You're almost there!

Congratulations buddy or budette: by completing the activities in your first trimester, you've nearly completed Brave Beginnings! Consider yourself a business owner of the first degree. By now, you'll have a considered business concept to bring to the market and a name for your business, and will have developed some basic understanding of tax and compliance and a healthy respect for contracts and copyright. You'll have at least thought about how you'll resource your business, and you've hopefully thought twice about quitting your day job.

This is really the most difficult Part of your 100 Days of Brave – and you've got it safely behind you! You've done so much heavy lifting conceptually, having tested your idea and committed to your business (and, more importantly, yourself). You can now move forward without second-guessing your decisions; you're going into your second trimester – Building Brave: Bringing Your Business into Being. This is where you bring your concept into the real world. It's such an exciting month of action and encouragement from the community that surrounds you (which includes the 100 Days of Brave Facebook Group, you know).

BRAVE ACTIVITY: Business ritual

Use the 100 Days of Brave Playbook and complete the Brave Beginnings Business Ritual. If you've not got it to hand, grab your notebook or your computer and write down the following clearly and with confidence:

· The name and by-line of your business
· What your business does
· How your business or offering is different from that of your competitors'
· What demographic and personality type your business will primarily serve
· Why your business is necessary
· Your referral partners
· Your vision for your business – where you will be in 6 months, 1 year, and 3 years.

Pro tip: don't um and ah over completing these questions. You've done the rumination already – now is the time to let the pen of the inner entrepreneur flow! Your experience as a business owner is one of almost continual pivoting – responding to the market around you is just part of the deal. You don't need to feel overly wedded to these answers, because they're not set in stone: they're simply a reflection of where you are right now.

You'll find many of the notes you make as part of this business ritual will inform your marketing collateral and copywriting. These preliminary 'cusp of entrepreneurship' notes are also delightful to look back upon as you progress with your business. They're also the foundation of many answers you might need to give to investors, real estate agents and banks!

Share your business in the 100 Days of Brave Facebook Group

If you feel ready, share your business with the supportive 100 Days of Brave Facebook Group! We're here to cheer for your new concept! Want to connect with the group in your city and have a celebratory 'cheers' for completing your first trimester? This is the place to do it!

Chapter 15

Things to know about your new life as an entrepreneur

The good, the bad and the ugly

Your life is gonna change, baby! And swiftly, too. You'll feel victorious, like an intrepid explorer. You'll feel freaked out and isolated, like a babe in the woods. You'll feel that sweet surge of adrenalin from making your first sale or landing your first client. You might occasionally be scared, but more often than not you'll feel proud. The fact is, once you put yourself out there as a business owner, people around you are going to have some feelings and opinions on the matter. They will fall into the following categories.

The good

When your besties gather around you and unconditionally cheer you on and support you for taking an exciting new step towards living an extraordinary and creative life, it's a wonderful feeling! They'll share news of your burgeoning business with their friends and employers, and name-drop you whenever practical. That's amazing, and they're excited for your success and development.

The bad

Your Mum or Dad might pepper you with questions about how you'll possibly have time to care for your children, or do your full-time job, or visit them each week if you begin your business as a side-hustle. Or they'll wonder at your experience and note 'how tough business is these days'. They might undermine your confidence with their own paranoia. It can be a direct deluge of negging, or it can be unintentional and couched as concern about your future. Either way, it's not helpful. I recommend nipping these conversations in the bud when you identify they're occurring and being frank about how their opinions on your entrepreneurship are unhelpful.

The ugly

When people from your friendship group don't approve of your change in lifestyle and attitude, things can get ugly quickly. People can become jealous, wondering why their friendship is no longer your number-one priority. They might make comments about how unavailable you are, or that 'you've changed'. Friendships don't always outlast changes in life direction – whether that's because of a significant new relationship, becoming a parent, moving interstate or starting a business. Breaking up with friends is sometimes part of going from one life stage to the next.

I appreciate that being cognisant of this doesn't make the process any easier. Breaking up with friends can be harder than breaking up with partners. I broke up with one very good friend when I really stepped into my identity as a business owner. It's irrelevant to go into details here – but my experience (and that of many entrepreneurs, male and female) is not unusual. Bottom line: haters gonna hate. If you've got to break up, you've got to break up.

*

That's it! I'm so proud of you: you've officially completed your first trimester, culminating in a business ritual that really seals the deal and gives you clarity on your offering. Celebrate with your tribe and get ready for your next trimester – Building Brave: Bringing Your Business into Being.

Part Two

Building Brave

Bringing Your Business into Being

Get ready to embark upon the exciting second stage of your 100 Days of Brave experience! Now that your foundation work is done, you'll spend the next month Building Brave: Bringing Your Business into Being. This is a SUPER-fun time, during which you'll be branding your biz, working with other creatives, building a community and bringing your offering or product into the real world. We're the midwives of our own destinies, and don't you forget it! Carpe diem, #amirite?

This second stage of 100 Days of Brave is all about LEGITIMACY. People want to trust the brands they use, whether those brands are single entrepreneurs offering an expert service, or rubber-duck salespeople selling squeakers to the millions. Legitimacy through branding, design and copy is what stands between a good business concept connecting with an audience, and abject failure. It doesn't matter how whizz-bang your business idea is – if you stuff up branding and get lazy with communications and marketing, you are heading for oblivion. We've all seen tragic LinkedIn profiles and Facebook brand pages that do active disservice to an individual or business. Upon observing the crappy iPhone photo with flash as their profile picture, and the odd assortment of personal and business images mashed unappealingly together, we wonder just how expert the self-proclaimed CEO or guru really is. Doubt seeps in.

Create a fortress of fabulous with legitimacy in the coming month, and you'll be onto a good thing. Don't worry about getting it perfect – every brand is a work in progress – but don't underestimate its importance and the consideration you must give to legitimacy NOW.

Chapter 16

Claiming your brand

It's yours. Own it.

There's nothing more aggravating (and expensive) than doing a whole lot of brand work – creating logos, building websites and making products – before realising that another business is already using your name… or worse, that you're infringing upon someone else's trademark. If you've read Elizabeth Gilbert's *Big Magic*, you might also be familiar with the concept of the 'gift' of a great idea. In short, Gilbert suggests that the Muse sends you an idea (in this case, your business idea) and that you MUST take action upon it. Tarry too long, twiddle your thumbs, and before you know it the idea will have moved on to another individual who will carry the concept forwards. This week, let the Muse know you're serious and that you mean business by claiming your brand – don't let that ripper idea get away from you!

Get googling and consider trademarking

If you've developed a relationship with a friendly lawyer during your first trimester, reach out to them in relation to trademarking your business concept. Trademarking protects your investment in intellectual property, branding and product development. Ask for your lawyer's assistance to identify if there are any other businesses (whether or not in direct competition with your own) using your proposed business name or selling a very similar product. Doing so now will avoid much heartache in the future! It means you can pivot and choose another name for your brand, if need be, before you drop heaps of money on creative. While you're about it, hop on the Google machine and get searching. Ensure to key your business name into major social media platforms to see if it is being used elsewhere by other parties, too.

Register your digital assets online

OK, you're sure of your business name and ready to proceed registering your digital assets! Yippee! Assets to register NOW include the following:

- **Your URL:** Even if you're months off actually building the website, register it properly right now. Get a '.com' or '.com.au' (whatever is most relevant for your location globally). You could chance it by going direct to GoDaddy or similar to register a URL, but as you'll need to connect your email to your website, I recommend contacting a friendly geek to set this up for you. It will save you tears in the very near future, I promise you. Please avoid the temptation to save a small amount of money by keeping your website a '.wordpress.com' or blog. Before you know it, you'll have a business... but you might find that someone else has registered your URL.
- **Your social media accounts:** Register your business accounts on Facebook, Instagram, LinkedIn, Twitter, TikTok and anywhere else you feel could be valuable. Prior to committing to the 'handle'

you'll use on each account, check what you are able to register across the main platforms. Your choices will be restricted by what previous account holders have registered as handles, and the length of your business handle. It's ideal to have the same handle for each social media platform – which isn't always achievable, but try your best. This means taking up the option for a BUSINESS account and not a personal one, which is particularly important when it comes to Facebook and Instagram. Having business accounts on these platforms allows you to advertise and monitor insights on your digital marketing campaign's success.

A note on the excitement of registering social media accounts: something happens to our itchy trigger finger when we register our business on socials. We want to share the good news with our pals and ask them to like our pages immediately. We're so used to sharing all our other good news that the temptation to share your business socials once they're live – even if they're not illustrated or complete, or a fair representation of the excellence of your offering – can be irresistible. My recommendation is to wait until you've at least got graphic design and branding basics in place before launching your business baby to the market. Delay gratification on this one – I promise it will be all the sweeter on launch day. Pinkie-swear it, and focus on getting your business ready for one helluva release to the adoring public. If you simply MUST release your brand prior to having an adequate landing page, use your logo to populate an Instagram business account. Post a couple of graphics-based teasers if necessary, but keep some mystery about yourself, gurl.

Here are a couple more handy hints about claiming your brand and building legitimacy:

· Please don't use a Gmail or Yahoo address for your email. Nothing says 'amateur' more than sallysbrownies@gmail.com.

Your friendly geek – or even WordPress or Squarespace – will be able to hook you up with a much more official-sounding crumbs@sallysbrownies.com email.

- If you're not asking a friendly geek to help you register your URL, consider using WordPress or Squarespace to set up your website until you're ready to recruit help.

Your brand brief and working with creatives

It takes a village to raise a brand.

Unless you're a graphic designer, a web designer, a digital expert, a copywriter and a photographer, you're going to need a small village of people to bring your brand to fruition. Don't get me wrong: I don't expect that you'll have the budget or inclination to drop a motza on all these creatives and experts in the coming month. But you should put in place a working timeline with hard goals for investing in the critical legitimacy-building assets you require to really make your brand win custom.

In my first year of business, I had my logo made, DL flyers and business cards made, and a website built. I worked with a graphic designer and a web designer to make this happen. While these things weren't cheap, they didn't cost me a bazillion dollars. I also had a blog, which I registered on my own.

BRAVE ACTIVITY: Locking your assets down and building your expert village

Set aside one full day on a weekend for registering what you need to online. Use this time to look for and connect with a lawyer if you will be trademarking a product or your name, and to source a geek to help you grab your URL and set up your too-legit-to-quit email address. Refer to your 100 Days of Brave Playbook for your digital asset registration checklist.

Then, set aside two or three hours to source experts in the categories of graphic design, website design, marketing, copywriting and photography to introduce yourself to. As you are unlikely to be spending money with them in the immediate future, be respectful of their time and make your stage of business development clear. They'll appreciate your frankness, and either catch up with you for an introductory coffee or simply send you their rate card. By being upfront about your startup stage, you'll be getting the quotes you need to budget and save for your brand's assets while developing a transparent relationship with your potential creative team. Once you have your preferred quotes in place, create a timeline for working with these experts. Whether it's 1, 6 or 18 months away, diarise it in a brand development worksheet. Use the Building Your Expert worksheet in your 100 Days of Brave Playbook – it has room to put all the details of preferred suppliers and the quotes provided.

Chapter 17

Logo love

Branding means legitimacy

I've noticed that some businesses feel they can go without a logo. Entrepreneurs making a product generally understand they'll need a brandmark or insignia, but sometimes individuals who offer a service (say copywriting, bookkeeping, cleaning or coaching) will try to avoid investing in an actual logo. This is a mistake. A well-designed, simple logo spells legitimacy for your customer. It sets you apart from the thousands of businesses who neglect to make this one simple investment. It gives you something other than a headshot or a basic font to use on your Facebook business page, Instagram, LinkedIn and Twitter accounts. You'll also use it in your email footer, on your business cards, in your newsletters, on your storefront, on your website... you get the idea.

Your logo: where to start?

There are a variety of ways to go about creating your logo. My recommendation is that you engage a graphic designer for this process, as your investment in your brand upfront means less likelihood of chopping and changing as you grow over the next year.

What makes a great logo?

Great logos:

- **Are simple and elegant:** They do not use a multitude of colours, or have fine or sharp edges as core to their design. A solid triangle in a block colour with a plain coloured background behind it is an example of elegant simplicity.
- **Come in two parts:** Your whole logo may incorporate both a brandmark and a font with your business name or a derivative thereof. It's important these two logo elements work well together AND separately, as long or unwieldy logos that incorporate text are difficult to utilise in marketing.
- **Are delivered to you as the customer in a variety of formats:** At the very least, you should be given two colourways (positive and negative) of your logo – featuring both brandmark and any text – in '.jpg' and '.png' formats. You should also be given '.jpg' and '.png' versions of your logo divided into the brandmark ALONE and the font ALONE. You might also have different colorways provided for seasonal promotions, again delivered in '.jpg' and '.png' versions.
- **Can be reproduced in various forms and retain their integrity:** Courtesy of strong lines, replicable colours and simple design, a great logo will be easy to reproduce in printed materials, online, and on t-shirts and products.

Crap logos:

- **Are bitsy and have heaps of detail:** A spikey sunray in multiple shades of yellow, orange and red is an example of a crap logo. As a brandmark, it is very hard to 'float' logos with too many contrasting colours and shapes over images. Reproducing complex logos in printed form is also a challenge. Stay simple, be cool.

- **Come in one long, unwieldy piece:** They're hell to work with, as you don't have the flexibility to present your brandmark OR your font separate to one another and this makes social media marketing taxing.
- **Are delivered to you as a file you cannot use:** Don't let a sneaky graphic designer provide you with an '.ai' file alone, or get away with providing just one '.jpg' version of your logo. That's practically useless as you start to play with your brand and need to use it in a variety of applications.
- **Have problems being reproduced uniformly:** A poor, overly complex design with a variety of colours is hard to reproduce in different applications. Its colours and lines will look distinctly different in the real world (say, on a business card or painted on a wall) versus the digital space.

How do you avoid getting a crap logo?

It all comes down to the brief. A brief is a critical branding document that provides your chosen graphic designer (and any creative supplier, really) with the information they require to interpret your desires and intentions. A typical brief document will ask questions about your brand and business offering, other brand identities you feel a connection with, and your values as a business. Even if you've not undertaken formal brand work with an agency (this is the process of clearly defining your brand messages, brand voice and values), you should know enough about your business purpose and the values associated with it to complete a basic briefing document. I can't overstate how important a thorough brief is: without it, both the graphic designer and you as business owner are scrabbling in the dark without clear parameters around the work to be completed. Your creative is likely to provide you with a brief document to complete.

Here are a few other tips on making your journey to 'the logo' a happy one:

- Have reasonable expectations about your working relationship with your graphic designer. They're interpreting your ideas about your business, and as such you might not connect with all their responses. This is actually a good thing, as knowing what you DON'T like brings you closer to clarity on what you DO. Similarly, understand how any edits are included in their quote for your logo and brand. Don't expect that you'll be able to endlessly reject the creative's ideas and have them come up with new iterations of your logo for the initial quote.
- Don't share the various logos you've been presented with in response to your brief on social media, or ask your friends for a poll on which design they like best. This makes you look like a hack – which you're not, of course. Your business is not a democracy. Have the strength and vision to make important creative decisions without listening to the Greek chorus, who are more likely to confuse you than provide you with valuable feedback. Behave like a professional, and keep your logo on the down low until you launch.
- While you're getting your logo designed, ask the graphic designer to expertly choose TWO fonts that will work with your logo. Also have them present you with recommended colour swatches you should use to accompany your font in the form of hex codes (they'll know what you mean).

With a logo, colour swatches and fonts at the ready, you've done the important foundational asset work to help all other creatives execute your brand. From website designers to sign painters, t-shirt printers to packaging designers, they'll have all they need from your graphic designer to bring your brand into the real world. Hooray!

BRAVE ACTIVITY: The brief

Set aside one-and-a-half hours to create a pre-briefing document of your own. By knuckling down and putting your brand vision to paper, you'll be in a great position to complete your chosen graphic designer's briefing document with clarity. Make detailed notes on the colours you imagine associated with your brand, brand logos you feel attracted to, how you think you'll use your logo (online, obviously, but also on packaging and promotional items if relevant), words you associate with your business, and the personality traits of your brand. A picture will soon begin to emerge!

Use The Brief worksheet in your 100 Days of Brave Playbook to begin the process of clarifying your brand design goals.

Chapter 18

Photography

Werk it

Businesses fail or thrive on their investment in photography. Whether you're selling tahini bliss balls or you're a psychologist, your customers make a decision about your legitimacy in a split second. They'll look at the images on your website and across your social media suite. They'll have a look at your product shots and zoom in. If you provide a service, your LinkedIn is going to be stalked hard. It's simple to ensure that your first impression is a good one: ya gotta hire a photographer to create images for you at least once a year.

I understand this can be challenging to hear, particularly if you're camera-shy. It can also be difficult to accept needing to pay for professional photography in an era when many of us have been exposed to the idea of DIY errythang. Great photography requires a talented photographer, not just anyone with a DSLR. Many's the time a client has come to me with a suite of images that a friend has taken with a DSLR – rarely are these images good enough quality to convey their brand message. If you want to nail that first impression, make that sale and establish your credos, you'll need to invest in photography, even if you can only get a small suite of images to begin with.

Planning your photoshoot

Great photography:

· Is naturally lit
· Makes you look like a human
· Captures the best of your products – both alone and in context
· Tells a story and conveys your brand values
· Is shot with a sense of purpose. Will landscape or portrait images best suit your digital identity? (Hint: I recommend more landscape than portrait for social media application.)

Crap photography:

· Is taken with a flash on your phone
· Looks poorly photoshopped and stiff
· Is full of harsh shadows and makes you and your products look cut-price
· Has no sense of context and places the subject in a void (for example, headshots taken against a white background as opposed to in nature, in your workspace, in a coffee shop, etc.)
· Won't work well on your website or social media suite because it hasn't been photographed with a particular function in mind. Be sure to brief your photographer on how the images will be used to avoid disappointment and additional cost.

Here are some ideas for your photoshoot:

· If you require headshots, avoid making them look like outtakes from *The Office*. If you're shooting in a studio, have headshots taken against soft, gentle-textured backgrounds lit naturally. Examples of these could include a white brick wall or a drop sheet of grey linen.

- Rally the troops! Have the photographer capture you with your 'clients' (who might be your real clients or your closest friends). You could be deep in discussion at a desk looking clever in glasses and gesticulating, looking Zen in your practice room (if you are a healer or masseuse), doing downward-facing dog in your yoga studio, outside the law courts conferring on a settlement, or leading a busy open for inspection. Whatever your profession, SHOW yourself in action!
- Want to make your products look irresistible? Go beyond the lightbox and create flatlays with your photographer, placing your products in context. Made a mean croissant? Shoot in your kitchen with beautiful napery and exquisite jam nearby. Selling a tent? Have photos of happy people snoozing gently outside it in the great outdoors.
- Go outside. Natural light and the real world make for compelling images, so nip outside into the back lane behind your business (or home office) and let your photographer embrace the urban. Work on a farm? Fine, have photos taken against the background of your beautiful crop or near the swaying trees.
- Walk it out. Motion makes for natural, easy images that offer a point of connection for prospective clients and customers. Have your photographer capture you and your team in motion on a stroll to the coffee shop, or on the high street.

A note on stock images

When you're illustrating your website and creating visual content for your social media suite, you'll need a large and varied library of images to draw upon. You'll only get so many photos taken in your first shoot – which is where stock images come into play. Stock images make most designers throw up a little in their mouths, but that's only because they've been overexposed to rubbish, generic stock images of the kind you might see illustrating naff business blogs. There is a whole world of beautiful, clever stock-image libraries that will support your brand vision and work in fine counterpoint to the bespoke photography you've purchased. Be selective, and subscribe to one or two stock image libraries you feel really connect with your audience. Whatever you do, don't copy and paste images from the internet or RG content on Instagram: this is copyright infringement as you do not have explicit permission to use the material, leaving you open to legal action.

BRAVE ACTIVITY: Paparazzi

Spend an hour researching potential photographers you'd like to collaborate with. Draw on the knowledge of the 100 Days of Brave Facebook Group and ask your tribe for referrals, too. Create a private Pinterest board where you collate images you enjoy the feel of – this will prove invaluable in combination with the Brief document developed in the previous chapter. You'll easily be able to explain to your chosen photographer the purpose of the images they'll be taking and the tone they must strike. Use your 100 Days of Brave Playbook to note quotes from your chosen photographers, so you've got all the information to hand when making a decision.

Chapter 19

Websites and blogs

This is your first impression. Make it count.

Your website is the first place most of your customers will experience your business. They'll make a snap decision about your legitimacy and pricepoint based on this key asset, which is why you must make it as appealing and bulletproof as possible.

Websites can be expensive – but they don't have to be. Simplicity in design and functionality should be your bywords in these early stages of your business development. Don't be fooled into thinking that simplicity of website use means simplicity in setting it up: the opposite is often true, so I recommend that you do not DIY your website for this very reason.

What makes a good website?

I've audited many clients' websites and can share the following gems of knowledge that will help you design a simple, legitimacy-building digital shopfront first go. Poor websites:

- Have heaps of text. Too much copy makes your website a drag for your audience. I know you've got LOTS to share about your business – like me, you can go on about all your unique selling points for some time – but your audience don't need to drown in words! Be clear and use simple, direct language. Edit that copy, cut it down, then edit it again. Now you're ready to go live!

- Look like crappy templates from 1995. If you have an old website you've grandfathered from a business you ran previously, do yourself a favour and start from scratch with a fresh, modern template you can amend to reflect your business.
- Have no social media icons or feeds integrated into their designs.
- Are clunky and make it tricky to make contact with you or buy your products.
- Are not optimised, and subsequently only look good on desktops. They're rubbish to navigate on tablets or phones, which is frustrating for users and likely to drive them away.
- Use colours and fonts inconsistently (for example, there might be one shade of blue on the landing page and a different shade on other pages).
- Have poor-quality photography that is inconsistent throughout the site.
- Have no pop-ups to encourage database subscription, letting potential subscribers slip through your fingers.
- Have a pop-up, but it assaults the audience before they've had time to gain an impression of your offering.

Great websites:

- Get to the point immediately. The audience know what you're selling, and fast. They're excited by your content and visit multiple pages during their visits.
- Are modern, streamlined and minimal in their aesthetic.
- Let images and branding do their talking.
- Have a consistent tone in copy.

- Make your social media feeds part of their design, with an Instagram widget or similar to show your level of interaction and keep things looking fresh.
- Make it easy for people to contact you to enquire about your services, or buy products from you.
- Are consistent in their use of colours and fonts.
- Encourage your prospective clients to subscribe to your newsletter so you can build your database passively.
- Engage with the 'Dark Arts': by this, I mean you've invested in remarketing to keep track of your customers as they journey around the web.
- Are easy to shop from and secure for your customers.
- Are optimised for both mobile and desktop browsing: so many of your customers will look at your website on the go – make sure their experience is a beautiful one that reflects your brand!
- Offer downloadable resources via an appropriately timed pop-up to an information-hungry audience in the form of ebooks.

Remember: a website is never truly 'done'. Once you've got that website as 'good' as it can possibly be – using my recommendations as a handy compass – don't continue bothering and clucking around it like a worried old hen. Websites are a work in progress and grow with your brand. I am continually improving copy and adding features to Ruby Assembly's website – it's just part of the landscape for business owners. Done is better than perfect!

Blogs and their import

Blogs are the very lifeblood of your website. They're really a non-negotiable, so build one into your website design – even if you don't feel like actually beginning your blog right now.

Still erring on the side of 'Why would anyone read my blog?' or 'I hate writing, can't I just trash this blog thing?' Here are some reasons why you should reconsider:

- Blogging regularly improves the magic organic reach of your website. Rather than paying a bazillion dollars in Google marketing, make your blog more relevant to Google by creating original content. The interwebs rewards you for it. Blogging well pretty much replaces the need for SEO (search engine optimisation), because you're naturally utilising all the words associated with your expertise in each blog. I don't use SEO to market my business because I'm always writing about social media, digital strategy and guerrilla marketing.

- Blogs show you're the real deal. Good blogs, that is. Don't buy packages of cheap content to bulk out your blog, filled with tacky stock images – they only serve to show potential clients how generic you are. By crafting good blog posts with a genuine opinion on a monthly basis, you're sharing your authentic voice with your audience. This is impactful, and over years of writing you'll have a large body of ideas associated with your identity.

- Blogs provide an appropriate space for you to collaborate and cross-promote with like-minded individuals and brands. Feature individuals you admire who might be of value to your audience, amplifying your organic reach through sharing in other communities. You may also be able to monetise your blog content, which never hurts, right?

- Having a blog means your audience can stay within your circle of influence for a longer period of time: why fill your newsletter with links to other news sites when they can explore your blog instead?

- If clients like what they read, they may well subscribe to your newsletter, or gift you with their email via a pop-up on your page. That's what I call database-building gold!

Still not convinced? Here, let me bust two often-touted myths about blogs for you.

Myth: you need to write at least one or two blog posts per week to make an impact

Wrong. You can enjoy terrific traffic to your website and social media suite by creating one really good blog a month. If you feel like writing more frequently, great! Go for it. A word count of 400 to 600 words per blog post is suitable.

Myth: blogs aren't worth writing unless you can gauge ROI on them

Pishtosh. Most marketing ventures do not allow for an accurate gauge of ROI. Think about adverts on the side of bus shelters or buildings; those gracing the glossy first eight pages of an edition of *Vogue*; the witty, compelling adverts played during the USA's Superbowl halftime break. None of these feature discount codes that allow the business to gauge how many packets of noodles, Italian court shoes or insurance policies they've sold as a direct response to the marketing investment. For some reason, the perceived measurability of the interwebs (hits, likes, clicks) has fostered an unreal expectation that you can gauge direct ROI from digital marketing. Digital marketing is a modern, targeted version of the bus stop, TV or radio commercial. Branding, particularly for startups, is about building trust and legitimacy. If ROI is your only justification for spending time and money on marketing activities, you won't grow a business. You'll just scrabble around in the mists of SEO and cheap blogs full of keywords that promise to give you ROI rather than committing yourself to the relentless, exciting, slow and magical process of building an audience.

Blogs give you a reason to reconnect with your audience regularly by presenting them with useful information or opinion each month. While they might have a 'call to action' to purchase or learn more, their key responsibility is to give back to the audience who follows you.

I recommend that you repurpose a blog multiple times over the period of a month to ensure that the biggest audience possible is exposed to your content. You can include a portion of them in your monthly newsletter, you can plan your digital marketing calendar around artworks that link back to your monthly blog, you can republish a portion (or all) of a blog in LinkedIn articles to enhance your credibility on that platform, and you can put budget towards social media posts that link to your blog.

What to write

The question that most business owners are stymied by is, 'What do I write about?' Successful blog posts are generally opinion pieces that answer a question, or posit a solution to a common concern. Whether it's reviewing lipstick swatches or talking about the five 'fails' most businesses owners make when leasing a commercial property, frank opinion is prized by the audience. Photography is also important, as is making sure you tag your blog with relevant keywords and hyperlink any businesses or concepts you mention in your article so the audience can explore further.

You don't need to constantly be 'on message' in blogs; selling at every opportunity is one sure-fire way to put customers off. For example, Ruby Assembly is a marketing agency, but the top three most-read blog posts on our website deal with egg freezing, divorce and online trolling. This means that my audience is interested in more than simply what we do as an organisation – they're interested in me as a leader.

BRAVE ACTIVITY: The website brief

Set aside one-and-a-half hours to create a briefing document of your own to share with your web designer of choice. What key functions must your website have? What 'dropdowns' would you like presented? Would you like your social media feed to be built into your website? Do you want a pop-up? Spend time gathering screenshots and URLs of websites you like, placing them in a Google Doc that is easily shareable with your creative support team. Make notes about each of the examples you include: WHY you feel it's a good website, HOW you think the website informs your own digital shopfront and WHICH elements of the website you'd like to incorporate into your own.

Use the Website Brief worksheet in your 100 Days of Brave Playbook to help you take notes and clarify your vision.

Chapter 20

Copywriting matters

Don't mince your words

Writing copy (text) is one of those funny things: most people think they can do it on their own. In the process of building a website, copy is routinely one of the last considerations. This is a mistake, as quality copy is as integral to your startup as having an appealing website. Often, business owners will create their own copy for their website. I understand why they choose to do so: they're spending money on a whole lot of other resources, and words are just words, right? How much better can a copywriter be?

The answer is much better. Much, much better. Poor copy is easy to spot: it breaks your hard-won legitimacy with an audience and comes between a brand's values and an audience's perception of your worth. You can have a beautifully designed website and a set of sweet-as images of your practice and your product – but if your copy is inadequate, there's an immediate disconnect. Common copywriting fails include the following:

- **Too much copy:** We've all got limited time in our day. Don't put a barrier between your audience and yourself by having too much copy on your website or in your ebooks. There is a direct correlation between large chunks of text and visitors clicking away from websites. Truly great copy is concise and full of – for want of a better word – flavour! Your copy should convey your brand voice and the information necessary in a succinct way that keeps your audience engaged.

- **Poor grammar and spelling:** Everyone knows a grammar nazi. But it's not those sticklers for detail you've got to write accurate copy for: it's for your garden-variety audience. They're literate consumers, even if they're not particularly literate themselves! They won't give you claps for writing great copy, but they'll sure as hell notice when you CAN'T write. Great copy is a bit like wiring inside a house: no-one pays more for it at auction, but if the power doesn't work (or worse yet, sets the house ablaze), no-one's buying at all. Avoid typos and grammar errors and your audience will accept you as legitimate.
- **A lack of clarity:** If you have a complex offering – whether that's a product or a service – less truly is more in the realm of copy. Too much information can be overwhelming and confusing for an audience. Pare concepts back and use the elegant minimum to explain yourself.

Great copywriting:

- **Conveys legitimacy:** We all know when we're on an amateur website. It looks like a template. It has loads of copy (and plenty of typos). Great copy educates your customers on your expertise and your personality as a brand or individual. It announces that you're the real deal and that you're ready to do business.
- **Sells your product or service:** Copy is iconic. Think of Louis Vuitton's 'Papillon' bag; the Apple iPhone; the Big Mac. These products have a life WITHIN the brand stable they've sprung from. These product names are intentional, magical pieces of

copy that convey a feeling, feature or brand statement. Such copy is powerful and motivating. It assists customers to incorporate your product into their imagination, connecting with the psyche on deep level. Great copy goes beyond the realm of features and benefits and into the space of consumer fantasy. Cha-ching!

- **Gives voice to your brand identity:** Your copy should convey who you are as a brand. Are you quirky? Straight-laced? Ultra-premium? Irreverent? Are you a disruptor, or a voice of authority and tradition? Your copy will communicate your identity with ease, supporting your great photography and graphic design elements.

- **Is written for your customer:** So often, belaboured, unnecessarily long copy is the result of 'copy by committee'. Too many cooks in the kitchen, concerned primarily with their own opinions, results in patchy copy that is written for the egos of the authors rather than for the most important person in the equation: the customer. If the copy clearly conveys how your product or service solves a problem for your customer, you're on the right track.

It's important that you engage the support of a copywriter or editor at this point. As part of your 'Building Your Expert Village' activity, you'll already have made a shortlist of creatives that should have included copywriters. Now's the time to reach out to these talents and see who will best fit your business, your personality as an entrepreneur, and your budget.

On working with copywriters and editors

Being a copywriter and editor myself, I can't overstate just how important CLARITY is when creating content for your website, ebooks, social media, and so on. Appoint a copywriter or editor who has a really robust briefing process. This might include interview time and a detailed briefing document you'll need to complete. Don't go cheap on spending time with your copywriter – the more they know about you and your audience and brand, the more accurate their edits and copy for you will be. Be very clear about what you want – you cannot expect your copywriter to intuit aspects of your business you need expressed. The corresponding activity for this chapter will help you connect with who your audience actually is, which will give your copywriter essential input on the brand voice they will need to create. In short, your copywriter can only be as clear on your service offering, audience and intention as you are, so engage in briefing properly and take time to prep beforehand.

BRAVE ACTIVITY: Who's your audience?

Set aside an hour and a half to create a vision board or written document that identifies who your audience is. You might even use Pinterest here if you are a visual person! Be creative and really let rip – the more of an 'audience avatar' you develop, the better your eventual copy and tone will be.

Here are some questions to consider:

- Is your ideal customer a man or a woman? Give them a name.
- How old are they?
- How do they take their coffee or chai?
- Where do they live, and in what kind of home?
- What's their favourite meal, or restaurant?
- What profession are they in?
- What is their income?

- What media would they enjoy? Think TV shows, books, magazines and podcasts.

Feelings of resistance may occur during this activity: you may find yourself saying 'but my product is for EVERYONE!' While this may be true, SPECIFICITY in marketing paves the way to success. You need to connect with your actual ideal customer here – it's time for magical thinking that results in concrete outcomes.

Chapter 21

User experience

Make your digital shopfront a welcoming place

The first place most – if not all – of your potential customers will visit is your website. Their reasons for visiting will be various: they'll want to see if they like your 'vibe', they may want to see what services you offer, to read your bio and establish your credo, to book a workshop or simply to see where you're located. They'll make a judgement about you and your offering quickly based on their user experience (UX). UX is effectively how the audience or customer navigates their way through your website, and it matters.

What does great UX look like?

Here are a few examples of great UX in a website:

- Clear copy and artwork that directs your audience to the information they need first; for example, buttons with content such as 'Our Hero Product', 'About Emily', 'Free Resources', 'Working with Tiger' or 'Services'.

- Uncluttered design and minimal, quality copy that explains your service or product.
- Abandoned shopping carts recalled from the customer's last visit.
- Pop-ups that invite the audience to swap their data for a valuable ebook or loyalty discount.
- A purposeful, attractive flow from product search to purchase.

Poor UX can result in lost sales and lost opportunities. Here are a few examples of poor UX:

- Too many tabs offering too many paths to find critical information on your product or service.
- Poor ecommerce design that fails to recall a customer's abandoned cart or previous purchase. This can be frustrating for the customer, who may consider several of your products for some time before finalising their purchase with you.
- Pop-ups that are difficult to click out of, or that obscure content or appear before the visitor achieves a sense of your offering.
- Auto-playing videos with audio that can cause embarrassment or irritation for the visitor (depending on where they are).
- A too-long landing page filled with disparate images, loads of text and no clear journey to purchase or engage with your service.

Your audience's UX is important whether you're offering a service or you run a store. Intelligent design for optimal ecommerce is critical in an economy where online shopping and sales via social media platforms are becoming par for the course.

Mobile agility

Your website must be mobile-optimised, as your potential audience is most likely to first encounter your website while on the go rather than at work. Many website templates will allow for mobile optimisation, but your friendly web designer's knowledge will be of value here, particularly if you're tweaking aspects of the design to get the most important information or products to your audience ASAP. Having a super-fancy desktop website is only half the game – if it presents as ugly or corrupt on a mobile phone, you'll lose credibility with your audience quickly.

Pop-up pros and cons

Pop-ups can be amazing when optimally used. They are your opportunity to gather critical customer data, helping you to build your database and learn more about your audience in one fell swoop.

Be warned, however: if poorly designed, they have the potential to destroy your mobile customer interaction and cause your audience to click away from your page. Bad pop-ups feel spammy.

Once you work out the purpose of your pop-up (whether it is to provide an ebook answering your customer's key questions or to offer a promotion or discount), implement it properly. Don't launch it until the 'back end' is connected to your database. Make sure the ecommerce powering your discount works. If you're choosing to provide an ebook, be certain that it's on-brand and provides great information and marketing punch. In short, ensure that your subscriber feels compelled to hand over their data – and feels positive about the promotion or ebook they receive in exchange.

Here are some pop-up implementation tips:

·   Don't have the pop-up appear immediately when the page loads.
    Give your audience some breathing room – let them establish
    your credo with around 20 or 30 seconds of exploring the site
    before you offer them a benefit.

- Make the pop-up attractive with good design – a generic pop-up will lead to lower levels of subscription.
- Ensure the pop-up is easy to get away from on both desktop and mobile. If you want the ESC key to take you away from the pop-up, this will need to be part of its design.

Privacy and data collection

Customer data privacy is a serious matter. If you've got an option for your audience to subscribe to a newsletter, or your website utilises cookies or collects data in any way, be on notice: you will need to have clear messaging around your use of cookies and customer information! This could be in the form of a pop-up or page on your website that relates directly to your privacy policy. Take advice from a lawyer on the most appropriate compliance adherence for your business. Think globally here – even though your customers may predominantly be located in one part of the world, the power of the internet means that your website will be visited by prospective customers from literally *anywhere*.

BRAVE ACTIVITY: Are you (user) experienced?

Take an hour to audit the websites of four businesses in your category that you think are market leaders. Follow your gut! Take notes on your experience of each website with fresh eyes, considering various aspects of design:

- What is on the first fold of the website on both desktop and mobile? What information does this brand expect its audience to demand first, and what can you learn from this?

- Are there any pop-ups or announcements relating to privacy or cookies? What data is being collected, and what is being given in exchange for this data? What, then, can you offer your clients, and what data can you expect to collate?
- How easy is it to purchase from the website? Does it feel safe to do so – and if so, what makes it feel secure?
- How are images and text used on this website? If they're effective, can you identify why that is the case?
- Are there any immediate 'calls to action' on the website? Does it invite you to subscribe for a benefit, or purchase based on a limited promotion?
- If it's an ecommerce website, will an abandoned cart be recalled upon reloading the site?

The Are You (User) Experienced worksheet in your 100 Days of Brave Playbook will help you clarify your vision, taking note of ways your own website can offer a positive UX.

Chapter 22

Social media

It's called 'social' media for a reason

Social media is the ultimate disruptor of commerce as we know it on planet Earth. Taking the concept of globalisation to another level, the power of social media platforms allows businesses (like your very own) to flourish from but the seed of a brave concept. In the old days of business, you'd have considered leasing appropriate commercial space to be one of the first items to tick off your to-do list. Now, entrepreneurs are investing first in proof-of-concept research, branding and creating the very best website and UX they can. Social media is at the heart of your customer's UX. It gives you unique access to your ideal audience by creating targeted content that is delivered to a distinct demographic. I really can't understate the competitive advantage this gives your business concept.

In the bad old pre-interwebs, pre–social media days, business owners would need to resort to expensive advertising investments such as radio or newspaper. They could hardly be called targeted forms of media, with potentially only a tiny portion of the audience being your ideal customer. Today, social media allows you to create relationships swiftly with your ideal audience, allowing you to market more effectively.

Before we begin unpacking social media best practice (yay!), it's important to acknowledge that social media is not free. Don't conflate the platforms themselves being 'free' with social media being cost-free. It's best to leave your resentment about having to pay to make your social media powerful at the door. Here's why: it's important to consider favourite platforms such as Facebook, Instagram and LinkedIn as newspapers that allow you to advertise your offering to your audience. Compared to traditional media, it's cents on the dollar to connect with your community – why should it be free? Budget for 'boosting' your material to ensure your investment of time in design and messaging is impactful; otherwise, very few customers will see your content.

Which platforms?

There are TWO possible answers here. One is a best-practice response, and the other is an 'I've only got so many hours in a day' response.

So, here's the best-practice reply: regardless of your business, you should be on Facebook and Instagram, and on LinkedIn as yourself and LinkedIn as your business. All the media you create should be shared on each of these platforms in the most effective way possible. The way you share content on Facebook is necessarily a little different to the message you will craft on Instagram (particularly in light of the use of hashtags on Instagram for growing your audience). Ultimately, ALL content you create should be shared on ALL platforms your business engages across.

Don't limit yourself by thinking your audience is only 'shopping' on one platform. If I'm a decision-maker from a large accounting firm, I'm on LinkedIn AND Facebook. As consumers of media, we don't turn off our interest in the world around us simply because of the social media platform we're on at the time. This is particularly important to acknowledge if you have a service-based business or a

B2B (business to business) concern: serious decision-makers exist on all social media platforms. It's your opportunity to reach out to them as many times as possible in meaningful ways.

Here's the 'I've only got so many hours in a day' response: if you have limited time available and can only handle one social media platform, utilise Facebook or Instagram. They're owned by the same parent company, and you'll have opportunity to advertise across both platforms simultaneously – if you can, please use both. When you're in startup, there are lots of moving pieces to address, and I don't want you to feel that if you can't do ALL the platforms recommended as best practice, you might as well forego the whole bunch.

Do what you can on a chosen platform at the best quality you can muster.

Services versus products: which platform is best for your business?

This is an important question to address! Sometimes business owners suggest that they are only wanting to connect with 'decision-makers', or particular roles within an organisation; they sense that an investment of time and resources into anything other than LinkedIn would be wasteful. Similarly, I have some ecommerce clients who only want to use Instagram, as they think their audience are only 'buyers' when on that particular platform.

Humans are multidimensional. We can be CEOs ready to recruit at the same time as being intuition-led babes purchasing essential oils and tarot cards. It is relevant for your business to be on Facebook, LinkedIn and Instagram, as your prospective customer exists on ALL platforms courtesy of being, well, human! You'll be surprised where your leads may come from, so don't limit yourself by having preconceptions about your customer and when their buying light is turned off or on.

How often should you post on social media?

You should post on social media a minimum of four times per week. You can share the same social media content across your social media suite over a week. This is a great 'starter' goal – it doesn't involve contacting your clients every day, but nor is it haphazard or risking leaving your social media suite dormant and your startup forgotten.

To make this commitment easier on your diary, you can opt to create all your social media content for the week in a two-hour timeslot. You can then use schedulers to stagger your content across the week – there is a wide variety of both paid and unpaid options that you can find online.

Be guided by industry-specific research as to when you should schedule your content to be posted. Facebook business pages and Instagram offer fairly sophisticated information on your audience activity; and in Australia, Sensis's annual social media report provides some great general information on when our community consumes most of their digital media. As a (very) general rule of thumb, posting during the early morning commute and after dinner means great exposure for your content.

What is good content?

Good social media is just that: social. When advising clients on their ideal mix of social media content, I'll often start with what social media ISN'T – which not only mythbusts a bunch of preconceptions about digital strategy marketing, but also gives pinpoint clarity on what NOT to do.

The key takeaway is this: social media is not relentlessly about you.

When many businesses first begin sharing media with their audiences, they want to make every post include a CTA (call to action). This is incredibly fatiguing for your audience (and for you too, in the long run), who want more from their social media relationship with your brand than being constantly sold to.

Imagine if you had a friend who only ever spoke about themselves to you, with scant regard for your interests or for discovering what was going on in your world. Before long, you'd find yourself rescheduling lunches and avoiding this self-centred friend. Don't let your brand become a bad friend to your audience!

The reality is that once your audience is following your page, they know what it is you do, broadly speaking. It is such a tough gig to grow your followership, and every new audience member is an achievement – don't throw your hard work against the wall by boring your audience with poor-quality visuals, relentless pressure-selling or narcissism.

The ideal social media feed is a clever mix of branded content and ugly, real stuff. The branded content – which employs regular, repeated use of logos and motifs, fonts and colour schemes – establishes the legitimacy of your business as a going concern. The ugly, real stuff (think selfies, and Facebook Live and Instagram Stories) shows your business 'off duty', giving you the space to show yourself as human and multifaceted.

Here's an example. Sarah runs a conveyancing practice. She has committed to creating seven posts per week, which she will share across Facebook, LinkedIn and Instagram:

- Three of Sarah's posts across this week will feature images of Sarah and her team, and focus on aspects of their service. This takes care of Sarah's branded content for the week.
- Two of Sarah's posts this week will be candid images taken 'on the go' during the course of her workday, while meeting with clients or at conferences, or in the form of Facebook Live sessions or Instagram Stories.

- Two of Sarah's posts this week will be 'discovery content' – material that may or may not relate directly to her industry but will be of interest to her audience more generally.

Pro tip: around 50% of your content should be on-brand, selling. Any more than this and your audience will begin to feel relentlessly sold to, and relationship-building will prove difficult.

Social media and copyright

Facebook, Instagram, LinkedIn, Twitter and Pinterest could be considered practically purpose-built copyright infringement technologies. They allow the easy and rapid sharing of other people's media.

As discussed in chapter 12, we social media users have been lulled into a false sense of comfort around copyright, particularly in the digital space. It is so easy to 'right click' or screenshot a cute quote or picture of Paris that will make for pure 'Insta fodder' that many of us forget all media has a provenance and copyright associated with it.

It is very important that your business respects copyright law at all stages of your development, but particularly in your startup phase. As a business, the onus is on you to be above board and to use media you've paid for. It's hard to build a legitimate business by stealing other people's intellectual property, #amirite? Develop good practices around media and create a brand that's truly yours using your own assets, or assets you have purchased or enjoy explicit permission to use:

- Only use media that you have ownership over, such as the images from your branding photoshoots. Don't forget to reference your photographer, acknowledging them however their agreement requires.
- Subscribe to a couple of high-quality stock-image libraries that will help you to illustrate other aspects of your business (for example, seasonal images, or images of people, cities or objects).

- If 'regramming' images, ask the owner for explicit permission and then take a screenshot of their permission. Be cautious, however: due to a rampant culture of copyright infringement, the person you've asked permission from may not actually be the copyright holder.
- Be cautious about using images from websites offering 'free' images. Various (and sometimes quite complex) licenses can still govern the use of these images. Better safe than sorry, I always say!

Connecting with your audience

I won't sugar-coat it: growing a genuine community of followers on social media is an investment. For your audience to grow, you'll need to invest time and resources into making good content. One of the real risks of social media is simply boring your audience to death with relentless selling.

Audience growth (and, consequently, sales and exposure) are related directly to connection. Like a real-world friendship, the audience expects a real conversation with brands. Sure, they want to know about your product and innovations – they want to feel your enthusiasm and passion. But they also want you to add value to their lives with fresh, relevant information (as per the earlier information on your ideal content mix). More than that, they want you to be real with them. This doesn't mean that you need to create a YouTube confessional channel that spills all the beans on your child custody arrangement, or your spat with a competitor. Ways to forge a stronger connection with your audience can include the following:

- **'Play along at home' activities:** These activities, which can include book clubs, recipe clubs or daily Instagram 'challenges', give your audience a chance to reveal themselves to you, while helping you to potentially attract new followers from their networks.

- **Real-world meet-ups:** Depending on your level of comfort around meeting in a public space (and the size of your followership and your personal influence), outings to the gallery, cinema or walks along the river can be a great way to connect. If you're concerned about numbers, you can limit the number of prospective attendees by running a competition to access the event.
- **Competitions:** Ensure you have the relevant licenses in place, first and foremost! Then set about creating a great competition with a prize people will actually want to win. In an era when we're becoming more security-conscious around data, the public will need a really great prize in order to hand over their personal contact details. Think broadly here: who can you collaborate with to offer a wonderful prize to your audience?
- **Workshops and classes:** If you run a service-based business, workshops are a great way to bring your business into the real world.

Return on investment and social media

If you're a number-cruncher, what I'm about to share next is probably going to hurt. If you're mad for the ROI report, this statement may dismay:

Reader, there is no true ROI on social media.

No, this doesn't mean that social media marketing is without value.

Consider this: what is the ROI on a double-page spread in *Vogue*? On a DL card drop? On your website? There is no direct metric for ROI on these media purchases – but that doesn't make them worthless.

In fact, the appropriate repetition of brand in creative ways is at the heart of social media's value.

In my business, I have this 'ROI real talk' conversation as early on as possible with clients. There are more than enough social media agencies who are happy to lie to clients about ROI, promising them thousands of Instagram followers and skyrocketing sales. Such agencies' model is quick turnover, churning and burning hopeful small businesses in their wake. This approach to marketing and customer care gives me heartburn.

In life and business – and social media – there is no shortcut to success and influence. It is true that you can measure ROI on distinct campaigns – for example, adverts with a special promotional code that allows you to see how many units of a product sold – but that is quite a separate project to the ongoing conversation you undertake on a weekly basis with your audience.

Social media is a kind of slow hypnosis (in the very best way). It reiterates who you are, what you do and what you stand for over months and years. By repeatedly exposing your audience to your brand, you plant it deeply within your customer's subconscious. This, the core function of social media, might be creepy to hear unpacked in so barefaced a way, but there it is.

Customers may take many years and many variations of exposure to your business to purchase from you, trust you and refer you on – and that's totally OK. In fact, it's the long game all serious businesses play. Retail businesses can more readily ascertain ROI on social media for consumer goods when running distinct promotional campaigns, but service-based businesses can't hope that a single ebook or social media post is going to make someone buy a house, purchase life insurance or invest in their education. What I want to impress upon you is that numbers will NEVER tell the full story of your brand's influence in the social space.

It would be convenient if they did – and some people will tell you that they do. In my experience, understanding your contribution to the digital ecosystem of your ideal client as 'minimum brand hygiene' is the most practical attitude to have. Fifteen years ago, small businesses were still umming and ahhing over whether websites were worth the investment. What, exactly, was a website's ROI? Those businesses who persisted in suggesting that the digital realm was a novelty that wouldn't impact upon the way they did business or marketed have gone the way of the dinosaurs. Those who focus overly on the ROI of social media, or neglect to create quality 'evergreen' content, will follow suit – but in far less than 15 years' time.

Social media to grow your database

When it comes to marketing your startup business, think like an investor in stocks: don't put all your client-loving communication resources into one category. While Facebook, Instagram and LinkedIn are highly sophisticated platforms from which to educate and cultivate your prospective clients, they're not YOUR platforms. At any time, the rules can change on a social media platform – they can make it more expensive to reach your hard-won followers, make particular kinds of promotions or competitions 'illegal', or simply shut down the whole kit and caboodle.

While social media platforms like Facebook, Instagram and LinkedIn are very unlikely to be disappearing any time soon, they regularly change the rules on their users. This doesn't mean you shouldn't invest in marketing your brand on those platforms (in fact, ya gotta, as those platforms are where your audience lives), but you should create content that helps you regain some control over your customer data. Think about your fave social media platforms as 'frenemies': they're part of your social group, but you know those shady bitches can go rogue! Do all you can to create digital assets for your brand that encourage your customers OFF their social media platform and onto your website, blog or landing page, helping you to gather their precious email data and build extremely valuable databases to power your startup well past your initial 100 Days of Brave.

Example: a risky social media strategy

Pressed for time, you choose to build your entire marketing strategy around Instagram. You buy followers to bulk your vanity number, and use bots to interact with your potential clients. You're getting lots of likes, but middling interaction – you don't truly have a great grasp on *who* your customer is.

Instagram chooses to 'block' your account one day, due to either an administration muck-up or your use of bots. Your thousands-strong social media asset, which you've spent years building and thousands of dollars of resources on, is now dead, and your customers have no idea where you've gone.

Example: a data-centric social media strategy

You choose to create content on a variety of platforms for your audience: you have a blog on your website; you have a landing page exchanging an ebook or one-time customer offer for their email address; you create content on Facebook, Instagram and LinkedIn. As often as possible, you create content that is more complex than simply a pretty picture: you draw your customers to your website or blog at every opportunity so you can collect their data in exchange for high-quality media that informs and attracts.

Facebook begin to charge you what you consider an exorbitant amount to share content to your followership. You flip them the proverbial bird and continue to share content on other platforms, as you're easily able to communicate with your core customers via your newsletter and other socials. One day you choose to sell your business, and extra value is attributed by your purchaser due to your sizable, clean customer database. Aren't you glad you chose a 'holistic' approach to your social media strategy?

You can utilise the following encouragements to get your audience off Instagram, Facebook and LinkedIn and onto your own website:

- **Ebooks:** An ebook is the most sophisticated data-collection tool available to your business, and it works powerfully for service-based businesses in particular. Create a beautiful, on-brand ebook that answers two or three frequently asked questions. Consider it a client gift, and understand that impressing your prospective clients with an ebook is the first step in building a business relationship. Plus, you get that sweet, sweet data!
- **Info-packed, entertaining blogs:** Blogging not only increases your organic Google ranking, it educates your audience and helps them to feel connected to your voice and brand. Having an easy 'subscribe' call to action helps collect that precious info, allowing you to build your audience data and ensure your audience is updated each time you post fresh blog content.
- **Linktree:** Instagram can be notoriously difficult to convert clients from. Create a Linktree account and create a shortlist of blog articles or ebook subjects you can send your audience to, direct from the 'gram.
- **Newsletters:** A good EDM (as we call 'em in the biz – short for 'electronic direct mail') will be rich with enough valuable content to encourage your existing clients to share it with their friends. Did you know that referrals are the most valuable form of new business? Newsletters are the bomb.

Facebook Groups and community curation

A Facebook Group wields more power and opportunity for organic audience reach than a Facebook business page could ever do.

Why? Because Facebook Groups provide a forum for your community to come together. Facebook business pages are ultimately social versions of your storefront – they're branded spaces where your followers can review and comment, but they cannot share discoveries and begin conversations. Facebook Groups give your audience the chance to socialise and share in the context of your business values. The power of this curated space should NOT be underestimated.

Here are some reasons to start a Facebook Group:

· You'll get more referrals.
· If you can convert these leads, you'll win more business.
· Your cashflow will improve, allowing your business to grow.
· Facebook Group curation can be a gaggle of giggles, and a great way to make new friendships and professional connections.

Here are some tips for creating a thriving Facebook Group:

· Don't replicate your Facebook business page as a Facebook Group. The Group needs to serve a purpose outside of promoting your offering. My Facebook Group Serious Women's Business: Northside supports female entrepreneurs to have robust conversations about entrepreneurship. It shares many of the values of my business, but it's not a place where I directly sell my service. At the same time, Serious Women's Business: Northside is clearly a Ruby Assembly–associated platform – which means I not only enjoy wonderful exposure to our 500-strong audience as a business leader and mentor, I get terrific referral business from it, too. Your Facebook Group must be a way to consciously give back to people who are ALSO likely to be your customers.

· Give your Facebook Group a distinctive name and logo: the more polished it looks, the more immediately legitimate and appealing it will be to your audience and their pals.

· Create content JUST for your Facebook Group every week. Once thriving, your audience will keep the conversation going with their own queries and comments – but as the owner of the Group, it's most practical to curate thought-starters that reflect your own values and interests.

Facebook Groups are a living petri dish of your followers! The whole gamut of society will appear as members of your tribe. Some will comment regularly, while some will be permanent 'lurkers'. Some will try and dominate the conversation, or relentlessly sell their own offering (which is why having clear Facebook Group rules is important). Some will fall prey to sycophancy and fall over themselves to be part of the digital 'in-group'. In many ways, a Facebook Group has the social dynamics of your garden-variety high school. Most members will be generous and helpful with knowledge sharing and referral – but it's up to you to set the tone and purpose of the Group.

A Facebook Group is for you if you want to earn more referral business and grow your brand faster. You'll take to community curation if you're a naturally social person who loves to share ideas and is curious about the audience they aim to serve.

It's not for you if you are obsessed with hard ROI and want to quantify time spent on fostering a community to your bottom line. It may also not be for you if you simply don't have the extra time in your week to concentrate on growing a group – you may want to wait 'til you feel more established.

BRAVE ACTIVITY: Calendaring one month of content

Focus on what you can achieve over the coming month around your business's social media output. Which platforms will you focus on? How often will you post? (To give you an idea, each month I commit to twelve social media posts for my business and eight for my Facebook Group.) Use the scheduler in your 100 Days of Brave Playbook, or devise a calendar on art paper. Expect things to get a little messy when you're in startup!

Real talk: the key to not feeling overwhelmed by your first social media strategy is to acknowledge that you can't do it all. Not in one month, at least! Social media strategy encompasses a full ecosystem of sharing, writing and branded content – it's a harmonious orchestra of media that develops over time. Once you've planned your social media activity for the coming month, you'll want to create a to-do list for social media projects you intend on completing beyond that point.

For more information on social media best practice, access Ruby Assembly's free Resources Library: rubyassembly.com.au/resources.

Chapter 23

Growing your customer list

The value of blogs, newsletters, ebooks, podcasts and workshops

The best way to speak directly to your customer is by building a mailing list. As explained earlier, putting all your effort into making content for one or two social media platforms is a risky use of time and resources. At any time, a change in algorithms can make you invisible to your audience. You could be locked out of your accounts through no fault of your own. Years of customer relationship-building can go down the drain in an instant. No joke.

Social media channels should be used to direct clients into your own digital ecosystem, encouraging them to swap their data for rich content that shares a bold opinion or expert knowledge. Social media platforms are a point of departure for your audience to engage with your business on your terms. Collecting accurate client data is the digital version of mining for gold. Your database provides you with a direct way to connect with your clients, decreasing your reliance on Facebook and similar platforms. Mailing lists are also worth real money, and add to the overall value of your business should you decide to sell it one day.

Here are the pillars of database building you'll want to engage with as regularly as you can.

Blogs

Give your audience a reason to stop scrolling their socials and to go direct to your website by writing great blog content, packed with opinion and expertise. See chapter 19 for more info on how to add a killer blog to your business's website.

Newsletters

Newsletters are the most powerful sales and relationship-building tool in your marketing artillery. They are simultaneously a privilege to send, and a risk – like all the best things in life, no?

A newsletter reminds your audience of your existence, connecting them with your offering. In the fast-paced world of relentless advertising, we are presented with thousands of messages a day – providing plenty of opportunity for customers to forget about you, or your service or product. For most businesses, a monthly (or fortnightly, if you're in retail and your stock is updating regularly) newsletter is critical for building customer awareness, sharing your values as an organisation and bringing on new clients or making fresh sales. Newsletters compel them to remember you, increasing the likelihood of sales, or referrals to your business. That's assuming your newsletter is a GOOD one, of course.

An effective newsletter that doesn't have your customer hitting the 'unsubscribe' button should amuse and educate, send followers to your social media platforms, and encourage them to view as-yet unread blog posts. It may also ready them to buy tickets to your workshops, purchase your new-release products or download your ebook. View your newsletter as a way of putting the work you've done on your blog, podcast, ebook library and so on in front of your potential clients' eyeballs again. All your existing brand rules, colours and logos should be used in your newsletter, reiterating brand and feel, which builds legitimacy. You can repurpose artwork you've spent time on already, such as materials from your social media suite. By reminding your tribe of your existence and the value of your service or product in a creative way that doesn't focus on 'squeezing' them or selling hard, you're winning at the monthly newsletter game.

An ineffective newsletter is visually incoherent and looks immediately 'templatey' and amateur. Poor newsletters have way too much text, or barely a smattering; they will be riddled with typos, and images obviously ripped from the internet; and their value will be undermined by a hard-sell approach. Not all newsletters are worth sending, #amirite? Poor newsletters can pose more of a risk to your brand than not sending one at all, denigrating your offering or (worse yet!) leaving your audience with the impression you're not the real deal.

Unsubscribes are a normal part of newslettering. Don't freak out or start castigating yourself when you see unsubscribes occur – there are myriad reasons why people unsubscribe. Farewell the old, and welcome in the new! The first time you send a newsletter – particularly to data that might be old – don't be surprised by a higher than normal unsubscribe rate.

Did you know that newsletters also give you rare insights into your customer's interests? Popular platforms such as Mailchimp allow you to see who has opened the newsletter, what they've clicked on and how many times they've engaged with your material. This is all amazingly valuable knowledge and gives you a 'to contact' list for your next round of prospecting!

Ebooks

The ultimate cold database-building tool, a well-written, beautifully executed ebook is one of the most powerful tools in your prospecting arsenal as a startup business.

It presents your customer with the chance to interact with you in a way that feels low-commitment and high-reward. It allows you to showcase your brand, offering and area or product of expertise – all of which are core to building passive rapport. Of course, it also serves the important function of helping you build a clean, accurate database that you can then go on to prospect with newsletters and offers. In short, make sure that a great ebook is part of your website and marketing plan.

What does a great ebook look like?

A great ebook:

- Presents knowledge or insight that genuinely helps your audience
- Uses all your brand collateral (fonts, logos, photography, colours, etc.; Canva has excellent ebook templates you can import your brand guidelines into, helping you create valuable documents that impress your legitimacy upon the reader)
- Has hyperlinks to connect your audience to your website, social media suite, or product or service
- Is filled with original images and feels like a coherent, professional document
- Positions you as an expert and the most desirable option
- Invokes feelings of gratitude and 'light-bulb moments'
- Connects directly to your database 'funnel' and allows your audience to begin accessing your suite of resources immediately.

A poor ebook:

- Is a narcissistic sales pitch that's little more than clickbait
- Is a ploy to extract data from your audience while jealously holding onto REAL information
- Is designed without a focus on brand, which makes the business look illegitimate
- Presents no opportunities for the audience to explore your digital ecosystem or offering further
- Is packed full of irrelevant stock images that clearly do not represent your business or offering as it is
- Makes the audience feel used and conned into giving you their data
- Sits alone, disconnected on your website, without funnelling emails to your database.

I can't overstate the value of ebooks to your business. Whether you're curating a beautiful ebook for your law firm or your reiki business, spending time on design and valuable content will result in an evergreen piece of marketing collateral that will impress your customers. Happily, it will also build your database! #Winning!

Podcasts

An increasingly popular way to share your brand and expertise with an audience, podcasts are a sophisticated marketing activity that takes time, thought, and a little bit of technical expertise to pull off. Having a podcast bolsters your legitimacy as a business, and provides a platform for you to introduce existing 'expert' clients to your customer base. There are great, accessible podcasting platforms for iPhone and Android that you can get started on, such as Anchor or Riverside.fm (which also records video, if you're thinking about vlogging). If you're looking for a producer to support you in creating a professional podcast, simply googling will put you on the right track. Apple Podcasts Top Charts, here you come!

Top tip: make your podcast sound professional by using a microphone and a small space to record if possible. If interviewing guests, use earphones to cancel secondary sound.

Workshops (real-world and digital)

If you offer a professional service, the value of workshops as a marketing device and soft-prospecting tool cannot be overstated. When I suggest to clients or mentees that they consider running a workshop, they're often intimidated by the idea. They feel that people might not be interested in hearing about their 'boring' profession, or that they won't have enough material to make a workshop valuable. In every case, this has been patently untrue! Workshops benefit your brand in so many ways: they give you content to discuss in the pre-event period, the potential of great images and feedback testimonials from the event itself, and the likelihood of business or referral from attendees. Talk about a virtuous circle! There's *no* downside to workshops; even if you don't end up running one, the marketing activity surrounding the project is worth the planning.

BRAVE ACTIVITY: #MarketingGoals

I know how overwhelming the workload of designing your marketing schema can feel. Let me tell you, it takes a client working with an agency like Ruby Assembly around 18 months to get all the pieces in place. So, take it easy on yourself; you're only human, and you need to commit to what is achievable and affordable.

Think about the next six months – what are TWO marketing investments you can commit to making? For many startups, they will be social media and a newsletter. I'd add a monthly blog to that as soon as you can, as it will give you an asset to link to in your social media posts and within your newsletter.

Here are some marketing investments for you to consider:

- **Newsletter:** What will you feature? What links will be provided to your audience? Which database will you use?
- **Blogs:** What will you write? How will you maximise your efforts across social media?
- **Ebooks:** Brainstorm and select a subject.
- **Podcast:** Consider if you'd like to try creating a podcast, and nominate guests you'd like to invite to feature.

To give you an idea, every month I commit to producing four original blog posts, one newsletter and one podcast episode. In addition, I focus on creating valuable ebooks that answer key customer concerns, releasing a new or revised ebook once a quarter.

Chapter 24

The Digital Dark Arts

Data-wrangling, SEO, remarketing
and Google Ads

Social media content is everything from Facebook posts to Instagram Stories, blogs to videos, LinkedIn articles to ebooks. In short, social media content is the high-quality creative elements that you develop to entertain your prospects and build a business. It is only half the story, however – to enjoy success from your social media content efforts, you will need to invest in what I fondly term the 'Digital Dark Arts'.

The 'Dark Arts' are the important, geeky parts of making sure that the content you so carefully curate is shared with the right audiences. Social media, contrary to popular opinion, is not free. It takes time and effort to create your content. And as I said earlier, social media platforms, along with Google, are best considered like newspapers: in order to reach your customer demographic, you will need to pay. Organic reach on social media is really a relic of the early days of digital. If you want to connect with your customers, you'll need to do more than create beautiful social media content: you'll need to devote discerning budget to it. And that's where the Dark Arts come into play.

Investing in a digital ad spend has various important benefits:

- Digital ads ensure your content is being delivered to your ideal client demographic.
- Clever Google Ads can increase your ebook subscriber rate.
- SEO content ensures your website is Google-friendly (though I also advocate creating regular, high-quality blog content for SEO purposes).
- Remarketing – my favourite of the Dark Arts – is a powerful way to re-engage website visitors with your business. For a nominated period of time, they'll be served advertisements about your business. If you're in ecommerce, for example, your customers could be shown their last unfulfilled cart and presented with incentives to purchase.
- Campaign-based advertising on Google, Facebook and Instagram drives customers to segmented 'funnels'. Funnels are a series of automated newsletters that maintain engagement with your client. The first newsletter might be sent when the client enquires about your service or product, the second automatically a few days later to check in on the client's decision-making process, and the last a week after that. Funnels do a lot of the hard work of following up prospects who need more time to make a decision to purchase.

I understand that much of this sounds like gibberish. Data-wrangling is a completely different skill to copywriting and marketing the features and benefits of your startup. Unless it is your major passion, I would recommend engaging a professional to help you with this important aspect of your marketing spend. Even if you only allocate a very small amount, investing in the Dark Arts will make a difference to your growth as a business.

BRAVE ACTIVITY: Delving into the Dark Arts

Spend an hour researching potential Digital Dark Arts professionals who can help you with this part of your startup journey. Draw on the knowledge of the 100 Days of Brave Facebook Group and ask your tribe for referrals, too. Use your 100 Days of Brave Playbook to note quotes from your chosen professionals, so you've got all the information to hand when making a decision.

Chapter 25

Collateral counts

Let's talk merch

One way of bringing your brand into the world is through an investment in merch. If it works for Taylor Swift and your favourite sports team, there's no reason it can't work for you! When I first began Ruby Assembly, I had some DL cards made up that (to my mind) were very fancy. They featured my logo, a very brief explanation of my core service, and contact details. I didn't drop them willy-nilly; no, I'd send them to prospects after cold emailing them, and before cold calling them. They were printed on quality stock, featured graphic design and made my business seem legitimate. It was my first foray into merch, and I can attest to the success of these items in building credibility.

Here are some beginner's merch options you might want to invest in, and how best to leverage the assets:

- **Business cards:** A no-brainer, really. You can design them yourself online, or work with your graphic designer for a more bespoke solution. It's important that your business card features essential information… but not TOO MUCH information. I recommend your name, title, mobile number, email and social media handle. Use icons wherever possible to limit the amount of copy.

- **Postcards:** Inexpensive and SUPER-powerful for prospecting, postcards featuring your logo and lifestyle images of yourself (or your product) are an absolute winner. They're the perfect thing to send after you've been networking, to follow up new business, or just to check in with clients you've not heard from in a while. I use postcards with photography of me and my team on them extensively, and the results speak for themselves.
- **Stickers:** Again, an inexpensive way of making any post you send look that bit fancier. Your logo on a gloss sticker goes a long way. They can also be used to 'brand up' gift bags or plain workbooks.
- **Tissue paper:** If you love client gifting, or you run a virtual or real-world boutique, branded tissue paper looks fancy AF and won't break the bank. It's easy to design your own online.
- **Apparel:** When I go to a conference, I tend to wear a Ruby Assembly t-shirt. Branded apparel doesn't need to be tacky, and mine is pretty minimal. I ask my team members to wear a branded tee when attending conferences if they feel comfortable to do so. I also have a rather excellent Ruby Assembly hoodie that is snuggly, which I wore around Europe shamelessly. I'm not silly enough to buy multiples of these items and expect my team to want to wear them in their downtime, but I do find that they're great for doing Instagram Stories in, and are a practical way for people to identify you and begin conversations at events. Creating apparel for your customers CAN make great commercial sense. If you're an influencer with a particular tagline, saying or theme, your t-shirts, hoodies, mugs or caps could be a nice little side-earner. If you run a store, or you sell a product that has a lifestyle or quirk factor customers love, branded merch could be a terrific fit for your business. This is the only proviso I have: do *not* give branded merchandise as gifts to your clients. Client gifts are about the client. Branded items are about you.

BRAVE ACTIVITY: Merch search

Spend a couple of hours brainstorming merch options for your business and researching potential suppliers. Draw on the knowledge of the 100 Days of Brave Facebook Group and ask your tribe for referrals, too. Use your 100 Days of Brave Playbook to note quotes from your chosen professionals, so you've got all the information to hand when making a decision.

*

You did it! In just one month, you've brought your business to life.

You little ripper. By working steadily through Building Brave: Bringing Your Business into Being, you've demystified the elements that make a brand recognisable, trusted and legitimate. By brainstorming through the Playbook, you'll have branded your business, collabed with creatives and really thought about what your customers need in order to take your brand seriously. Methodically and with purpose, you've done what many other businesses fail to do: enquire strategically about what your brand is and how it can best communicate with its paying audience.

Bravo, you good thing. You're too legit to quit. It's time to celebrate in your favourite Facebook Group, and to get your friends together for a brilliant brunch or hectic drinks session. By Jove, you've earned it.

Part Three

Being Brave

Working in and on Your Business

Oh, you lucky, lucky thing: you're on the home stretch! By this stage of the 100 Days of Brave project, you've done the deep work necessary to establish a viable product the market has an appetite for. You're now a compliant business owner with a legit brand. Now comes the fun bit! You get to work IN your business and ON your business – both of which should be an utter pleasure and reward.

I am literally rubbing my hands together in excitement for you! In this closing portion of the adventure, you'll learn how to prospect and win business from scratch without feeling icky. You'll develop a strategic marketing plan and learn to manage your emotions around negative feedback. You'll begin networking in a way that feels right for you, and develop strong referral relationships that represent a virtuous circle of commerce and culture. To cap off this festival of fun, you'll be curating a business launch party to write home about.

Boy oh boy. Get ready for the good times, and let's get your business show on the road! It's time to embrace Being Brave: Working in and on Your Business.

Chapter 26

The charm offensive

Gratitude is the good oil of life

It feels good to express gratitude, and it is wonderful to learn that someone else is grateful for your efforts. A significant amount of business success can be attributed to expressing gratitude: to our teams, to our customers, to our families and friends, to our referral partners and even to our clients-to-be. Taking action on gratitude will benefit your business long into the future. Here are a couple of ways to implement gratitude into the pattern of your daily business doings.

Hi, thanks, good to meetcha

One way to show gratitude to your clients is by sending them thank-you postcards or gifts. Here are some situations in which you might want to send thank-you postcards:

- You've just finished up at a networking event or conference and have a stack of business cards in your hands. After adding these new contacts to your database, delight them with snail mail.
- You want to say thanks to a new online (or real-world) customer.

- You want to follow up prospecting activity with a piece of cheeky snail mail.
- A potential customer has made an introductory enquiry about your services.

Here are some situations in which you might want to send thank-you gifts:

- You've been referred a potential customer. (Don't wait 'til you've won the business – gratitude isn't conditional!)
- Someone has just become a new client or customer. Be smart and scalable about this. If a client has just signed a 12-month contract, their gift should be different in value to someone who has made their first purchase from your e-boutique.
- A special client anniversary or happening has occurred. Perhaps they settled a home, had a baby, got married, got divorced, or moved into new business premises. Acknowledge your client's big life moments.

Client Love Day and seasonal gifting

Gifting as a way of showing gratitude is core to my values. As an entrepreneur, I feel very passionate about expressing joyful thanks to clients. After all, it's due to their trust in my service that I have a business and can employ staff. Having come from a real estate background, I've seen PEAK lacklustre gratitude materialised in the form of naff branded gifts that are all about the business and not at all about the customer. If you've just dropped $900,000 on a house, is a branded cheeseboard and a cleanskin bottle of wine REALLY the best way to thank you?

I have three key gifting periods annually in my business for existing clients. They need to be shown that you love 'em and value 'em! These are:

- **Client Love Day:** THE most important date on the gifting calendar, Client Love Day is your opportunity to surprise and delight. Arriving out of the blue, Client Love Day sees my clients receive a veritable Santa sack of treats delivered to their business. These are generous and themed; they don't necessarily cost a motza, but they do take time to organise. This is where the value lies: you've taken time to create a delightful surprise for your client. Themes I've curated for Client Love Day in the past include 'Winter Warmer' (a soft blanket, book, mug, tea, journal and pen) and 'Summer Holiday' (cheeky gin and tonic cans, a beach towel, sunblock and a novel). If you feel that your diary is too full to execute this task yourself, outsource to a team member or use a great gifting company. The important thing is that this treat surprises, delights, and feels personal.
- **Easter or Greek Easter:** I send my clients a holiday gift, which is often a traditional Greek Easter bread, a beautiful Ruby Assembly card featuring an Orthodox icon, and a white, red and blue candle. This is a highly personal gift from me to my clients, and is courier-delivered. I think it's important that we share aspects of our own lives with our clients; it brings everyone together.
- **Christmas:** I have a couple of Christmas gifting activities. I hold a Ruby Assembly Feast for those who can join me and my team at lunch in very early December. I love coming together with my clients around food; it's a great way for me and my team to feel part of something bigger. Seeing my clients interacting and laughing and celebrating together is priceless. Naturally, COVID-19 has impacted on my ability to hold such an event of late, but I have faith it will be a fixture again in the future!

For those who can't make it to our Feast, I send a Christmas gift. They are often themed presents: one year we created boxes packed with treats from team Ruby Assembly's countries of origin. There were Dutch biscuits, HP sauce from London, Greek beer and Italian pasta. The level of detail in these gifts does depend on the time we've got in the lead-up to the holidays, but a Christmas gift always goes out!

BRAVE ACTIVITY: Plan for gratitude

Spend an hour brainstorming how you'll express client gratitude using your 100 Days of Brave Playbook or business diary. Depending on the nature of your business, you'll want to consider:

- bespoke thank-you cards
- referral presents
- gifts with purchase (virtual in the form of a discount or an ebook, or physical)
- anniversary gifting
- seasonal gifting
- your own version of Client Love Day.

A note on budget

While budget always plays a role in gifting, I am adamant that there are ways to express gratitude to customers and potential customers without breaking the bank. When I first began my business, I had very little money and chose to handwrite thank-you cards (sometimes with the addition of $1 scratchies!). The point is, don't get lazy with gratitude and gifting. You can do it, your business will grow courtesy of it, and you'll love being able to spend more on your clients as you thrive.

Chapter 27

Know your ideal client

You don't need to be everyone's
cup of tea

One of the biggest barriers to business growth is time wasted on ineffective marketing. This costly wastage stems from a business owner's lack of enquiry into who they understand to be their ideal client; instead of diving deep into who they WANT to be their customer, they go wide and attempt to appeal to everyone. That way, reader, failure lies.

It can be tricky to identify your ideal client when you're in the startup phase of business. Narrowing down your audience can feel self-limiting, as though you're curtailing your business before it has yet grown. 'My product is for everyone', you might think. While it COULD probably be for everyone, it is more likely primarily for a particular group. I suggest that you initially focus on two ideal audience groups to begin with. You may be tempted to identify and aim for more, but please resist the temptation. Once your business is up and running there'll be time (and resources!) to expand your audience focus; at the moment, though, we're looking to get super-focused on appealing to your core clients.

How audience segmentation supports prospecting

Focusing on particular client categories is definitely part of the 'secret sauce' of my business's success and renown in specific sectors. I've built marketing content tailored to distinct groups I'd like to work with almost since day dot. (This was intuition, rather than strategy!) I began by building a 'list' of real estate clients and became a go-to for digital strategy in that sector. My growing reputation in real estate marketing also led to me to serve 'adjacent' businesses, such as real estate–centric software developers, photography agencies and complimentary outsourcing businesses (such as accountants) that focus on the property category.

I then decided I wanted to expand into new territory, and so I began to build a legal list. I had already gathered a few law firms to Ruby Assembly, and my team and I enjoyed working in the legal space. Lawyers were way more fun (and far less frightening) than we imagined at first. Why shouldn't Ruby Assembly try to win more legal business, too? I decided to build media that focused on lawyers and their major marketing concerns, and our reputation in that category began to flourish. Growing a business truly is a lot like gardening: identify what will thrive in your garden and support those plants to burst with life.

There are two main reasons why tailoring your offering to match the needs or preferences of specific groups is a powerful marketing strategy:

- Defining a core audience directs the way you use your time 'on business'. Whether you're selling beach balls or wills, focusing on audiences you feel will be most receptive to your product helps you get deeply intentional with your marketing. When you're a newbie business owner, time is a finite and valuable resource. Spend it on marketing to people who will spend with you. Attempting to appeal to everyone slows momentum and makes it harder to know where your time is best spent. Filling your ideal week with core marketing activities that support your target audience and build your reputation is only achieved by knowing your goal, and that's appealing to your core audience of ideal clients.

· Appealing to distinct audiences helps you to become a 'hero'. Many categories of society feel unspoken to, or are in an information-hungry period of their life. By looking at the needs of your ideal client, you can tailor communications, launches, service solutions and products to address their interests and concerns. This isn't brain surgery, and the categories don't have to be niche or groundbreaking; knowing that you want to appeal to parents of newborns or families with tweens provides tons of communication opportunities. Once an audience understands they're being directly spoken to and supported by your business, the organic growth and sharing of your offering begins. Your reputation as the 'go to' or 'must buy' for this particular audience begins to grow – and that's where the money and momentum is, honey!

BRAVE ACTIVITY: Vox pop 'em

Want proof of concept when it comes to your core audience? The process of identifying your 'best earning' customer market is not dissimilar to our initial activity of proving there's a desire for your offering. Much of the work you did in Part One of 100 Days of Brave will inform your initial audience focus; your intuition is probably ringing loud and clear about the two markets who'll love you best.

Still feeling unsure? Dive deeper for social proofs:

- Set up a survey on SurveyMonkey of no more than eight to ten questions. If possible, avoid yes/no questions – look for short comments so you get a bit more knowledge from participants.
- Send this to your community of friends and family on social media, and ask them explicitly to support you by answering.
- Post the survey to Facebook business groups you participate in.

Chapter 28

Prospecting ain't a dirty word

Do the difficult thing, and it becomes easier

If there's only one key thing you take away from Part Three of *100 Days of Brave*, it is this: businesses that do not prospect fail. Many business ideas have merit, and I've spent time mentoring amazingly enthusiastic, well-meaning and kind people as they start up or seek to grow their brand, but no amount of goodwill or enthusiasm will make up for a lack of business development. Products do not sell themselves to audiences without marketing intention – their owners must take time to put their product or service in front of their audience regularly.

I know how uncomfortable the idea of business development is to many. Many would-be business owners squirm when I begin discussing prospecting. 'I hate selling! It's just not me', they say, or, 'Prospecting feels so tawdry. I don't want to call people or disturb them like a telemarketer'. My question to them is this: do you want a business, or not?

No prospecting, no business. Whether you flourish in entrepreneurship or not relies so much on your attitude towards sharing your offering with others. Will you be shy, or scared of others' judgement about sharing your venture? Or will you work to amend your attitude of reticence so you can enjoy success and provide support to the widest possible variety of customers?

How I overcame prospecting cringe

When I was a real estate agent, I was put on the phone to 'prospect'. This meant making those calls after an open for inspection to see if a guest would like to buy the property, and to learn more about what they might need. I would make 50 to 100 of these calls a day, initially. When I began cold calling, I am sure I sounded nervous. But as I made more calls, the sheer volume made me care less about rejection, and also view my role as helpful rather than intrusive.

Your attitude to prospecting makes all the difference to your success. At my core, with my first experience of prospecting, I eventually came to feel that I was doing the customer a favour by calling them. I was extending a courtesy to them – I believed they were LUCKY to receive a call from me. This shift in attitude certainly impacted on my positive 'hit rate', and I'm sure it also buffered me against the occasional rudeness I experienced. Here's the thing: far fewer people will be rude to you as a business owner attempting to do business development than you might dread. And the great thing is, if anyone is rude or gives you a bad vibe, it's a self-sorting mechanism! You simply delete them from your database or phone list and focus on connecting with more clients who need your service. Next!

I continue to prospect to this day, enhancing customer lists I've cultivated for years, introducing myself to people I'd like to do business with and designing new content for new categories of client I'd like to support. Prospecting is never 'done'. It's just like sunblock – you need to apply it daily! And the surprising thing about business-building and reaching out to new customers is that most people are pretty darn nice about it. Go on, surprise yourself with a bit of prospecting!

My prospecting process

I've always been very transparent with communicating the methodology around prospecting. That's because I feel that there is more than enough work available for all to enjoy, and that most people probably won't undertake this process. As I hope I've been able to show you throughout your 100 Days of Brave, building a business isn't brain surgery. It's small steps, taken with care, done regularly. That's it. The process I describe over the next few pages is ideal for newbie business owners who've not done business development before. It requires a few bits of collateral to execute it with maximum impact, but you should have most of the assets described after completing Part Two of our journey.

Step 1: Who shall I contact today?

I introduce my business to new clients in a couple of different ways. I'll either decide I'm going to work on growing a particular 'list' that day (lawyers, for example, or coaches), or the approach will be more reactive (I've noticed a business I think would be a good fit for Ruby Assembly).

If I'm focusing on growing a 'list', I'll look to find a central resource I can work through. For example, if you run a professional service wanting to speak to doctors (or lawyers, or hairdressers, or software designers), you'll want to find an 'institute' or guild website with a central database. Alternatively, you can just google 'family lawyer in Melbourne' or 'hairdresser in Sydney' and a bevy of prospects will appear before your eyes.

Once I've got a list, I spend time visiting potential clients' websites to learn a little about them. Do I get a good vibe from the website? Does their website indicate they might need my help? What can I note from their online identity that I might highlight to them in my introduction? Note that I don't rush this process. I want high-quality prospects that are likely to find my business values appealing – not every listing on the internet.

Step 2: The email

When I decide to reach out to a prospect, I find the email of the director or owner of the business. If there are multiple parties presenting as senior, then I'll include all of these individuals in my introduction. To avoid your introductory email being deleted or ignored as spam, it's important to tailor it as much as you possibly can to the client. Here's an example of a useful introductory email:

SUBJECT: [Your business's name] x [prospect's business's name] (people are always curious to see their own name or their business's name!)

Dear [first name],

A note of introduction. My name is [first name], and I'm the [title] of [insert business name].

I've been observing your business on social media for the past couple of months and thought that now was a good time to reach out to you. [Business name] is clearly respected in its field, offering [service or product type] to your customers. I can see that there is opportunity for you to [make general but accurate suggestion about improvement based on your observation of their business].

My business, [business name], specialises in [service or product type]. [Explain how you do what you do, and a value you employ in your execution; for example, Ruby Assembly specialises in social media for professional services, making even the most complex or difficult communications entertaining and interesting for your current and prospective customers.]

I'm attracted to your business and sense we may work well together. I attach a link to our ebook/blog [relevant ebook or blog link] to demonstrate our leadership in this category. I trust you will find some nuggets of value therein.

I welcome you to our studio to discuss how our two businesses might collaborate.

Best,
[First name]

And there you have it. Short, packed with observations that will impress your prospect, and far from sounding desperate for business. There are several reasons why this introductory email is so successful, but its value hinges on how many tailored touchpoints sit within it. The intended recipient will see that you've taken time to explore their business and respond to their brand, unbidden.

The most important element of this email is the link that is ideally tailored to the prospect's interest or work category. When prospecting a lawyer, I will send a link to an ebook that is specifically tailored to a lawyer's pain points. If prospecting a 'random' that doesn't fit into any particular list, I will send a general ebook that I call *Social Media SOS*. In order for the prospect to read the ebook, they must subscribe to our mailing list, which is the CORE PURPOSE of this email. You want to show interest, share knowledge and welcome them into your marketing vortex.

Step 3: Snail mail and 'lumpy mail'

Directly after sending this email, I handwrite a Ruby Assembly postcard and pop it in the mail. It's important that the postcard looks personal in some way. I use postcards with team photoshoots on them rather than a logo, which would look too businessy. I write a personal message expressing enthusiasm for the prospective client's business or project, and reiterate that I'm looking forward to meeting with them.

I like sending a little gift when possible, too. This is known in the marketing world as 'lumpy mail', which is again more likely to be opened by the intended recipient than by an administrator. I pop in a branded Ruby Assembly face mask, or a USB stick, or simply a scratchie – something little that is inventive, unexpected and delightful.

Step 4: LinkedIn

I look up the prospect on LinkedIn and add them.

Step 5: Diarise follow-up

I diarise to email them a courtesy follow-up within a month, which again includes the link to the ebook so they might subscribe to our mailing list.

*

And that's it! That's the secret sauce of my initial prospecting process. After a client has received five touchpoints of courtesy and curiosity in the space of a month, you're taking that prospect from 'cold' to 'warm' – which means if you call them, they're probably going to know who you are. The efforts you've made certainly put the weight of goodwill behind you and make outright rejection far less of a possibility.

I hope this process makes you feel more in control of business development, and less scared of being rejected. While cold calling can certainly be a part of prospecting, there are many other meaningful ways to connect with potential customers, as this five-step process illustrates.

Here are some tools to make prospecting easier:

- **Ebooks:** Your first priority when building a library of downloadable resources is to curate a general ebook that will appeal to most customers, and then look to build two more that address the concerns of your two core client lists. For example, at Ruby Assembly our general ebook is *Social Media SOS*, and we also have *Social Media for Lawyers* and *Social Media for Estate Agents* downloadable on our website. Having these tailored ebooks ready to go is the key to unlocking a relationship with a 'cold' prospect. You want to curate a document that feels like your brand while answering four or five genuine queries, or presenting four or five solutions. This will make it easier for them to give you their contact details, allowing you to communicate with them regularly via a newsletter.

- **Postcards:** A multi-tiered prospecting process needs to feel human; by sending a non-branded postcard that piques curiosity, you're on the way to building a relationship. You can use the images you've had taken for your website as the basis for these postcards, and there are plenty of inexpensive printers to order from online.

- **Smart branded items:** Reciprocity starts with a li'l generosity! Useful branded items that you can pop into an envelope along with your introductory postcard include flat USB cards, face masks and computer webcam privacy screens. I've founded that $1 scratchies and a little bit of glitter work just as well in the 'first impression' stakes, too.

Marketing versus prospecting

Many business owners conflate marketing and prospecting, and I can see why: both are ostensibly outward-facing activities seeking to engage with customers. Marketing and prospecting are both essential elements of your business activity pie, but they are different, and they impact on your growth in unique ways.

Prospecting is about introducing new people to your brand, while marketing is more about creatively putting your business or product in front of customers who already know of you. They work hand in hand, particularly with small-scale startups, which may be time-rich but light on funds. You need to introduce people to your brand before you're able to repeatedly market to them.

BRAVE ACTIVITY: Ready your ideal prospect email

Use the basic prospecting email provided in this chapter as a foundation for your own client email. If you're selling a B2B service, think about business factors they may benefit from improving or optimising. If they're a retail client who has joined your mailing list, consider the interests they may have. For example, if you're selling a maternity bra, you may create an ebook that focuses on easy styling hacks for new mamas. So long as you're writing material that addresses a need of your prospect, you're on the right track.

Chapter 29

Developing your prospecting and marketing calendar

Prioritise your important plans

At the start of each year, I use a planning tool to help me put the 'big rocks' I need to achieve in place. If things aren't made space for, they tend not to happen! My 'big rocks' are my necessary personal and business-related goals. In terms of wellness, they include a week 'out' of the business every two months, a monthly trip to the hot springs with my husband, and time for two or three workouts a week. When it comes to business, my core priorities are weekly prospecting, monthly blogging and vlogging, monthly podcasting, monthly newsletters and quarterly workshops. Do all these 'big rocks' get ticked off every month as planned? Hell no. Life gets in the way. But if I've made the space for my personal and commercial needs to be met, they're THAT MUCH more likely to be achieved.

What do I use to help me identify my priorities? It's usually a business planner (my favourite is Leonie Dawson's duo of *Goal Getter Yearly Business Workbook* and *Goal Getter Yearly Life Workbook*), a calendar and my Google calendar. I don't usually complete these extensive planners, but I don't punish myself for that, either. They serve the key role of helping me review what worked in the previous year, what I'd like to do this year, and when I'm going to do it. Once I have my new-year calendar lying before me, I block out my most important personal, prospecting and marketing activities in coloured ink and on my shared work calendar.

Considerations when planning include the following:

- If you run a product-based business, are there particular sales cycles you need to prioritise marketing around? Examples could include Black Friday, Boxing Day or Valentine's Day.
- If you're running workshops, is there a day of the week or a time of day that will be better for your students?
- If scheduling social media or newsletter content, evening is best for maximum organic reach and enthusiastic open rates.

BRAVE ACTIVITY: Your prospecting calendar

Using the 100 Days of Brave Playbook or your own calendar resource, divide your prospecting and marketing goals across 12 months. Don't forget to leave room for holidays and personal priorities! Once you know in which month you intend on completing which prospecting and marketing activities, get specific and block out the days when you intend on finishing these work items.

The sickest 100 Days of Brave prospecting playlist

Pump up the jams (and build up your database) by spinning the official 100 Days of Brave prospecting playlist on Spotify: https://open. spotify.com/playlist/5JfInsMQIUKwhqWhbyYrBe. BPE (big prospecting energy) guaranteed.

Chapter 30

Ouch, that hurts!

Overcoming rejection

I always think that a large part of being successful in business is RELENTLESSNESS. Happily, it is a quality I have in spades, but I appreciate not everyone is as 'like a dog with a bone' as I am. Many businesses fail to flourish because their owner is afraid of being rejected by a customer, or they're put back in their box by well-meaning but unhelpful feedback from a family member or friend. This stops them going out and doing 'real-world' things like networking, holding Facebook Live sessions, running workshops, presenting at trade shows and the like. This ultimately prevents them from growing their business, which is a shame.

Here's the thing: being in business isn't necessarily brain surgery. It's turning up (pretty much) every day and doing what you say you do. You bake every day with a specialty in camp cakes? You're a baker. You consult with teams at local councils? You're a facilitator. You write blogs about horticulture? Great, you're a writer. The sheer number of hours you put into your business will naturally help you to level up as you go. It also means you'll be having interactions with customers, suppliers, contractors, landlords and staff.

Here are some things to remember when receiving rejection or tough feedback:

- 'No' doesn't mean 'no, forever'. It could just as easily mean 'not right now', which is actually an opportunity to begin building a relationship with a future customer.
- Not every customer is a good match for your business. You don't need to solve everyone's problems, or be approved of universally. You're allowed to have standards, and you're no-one's doormat.
- Rejection or rude feedback is actually a helpful waymarker from the universe. Unsubscribe, reject, delete that customer!

Of course, feedback is one of the ways we improve as business owners. We just need to be selective about whose feedback we take on board, gauging if it makes sense for our values and business model. Here's an example: a few years ago, I was referred to a client who was a professional bloke in his late 50s. He was successful, and had run and sold a couple of businesses; we got along very well at our meeting and there appeared to be a great synergy between us. Duly, I sent him a proposal. A couple of days later, I received a surprising email that said how disappointing he found the proposal, and how unprofessional it was in comparison to how I represented my business as a person.

I was shocked, and I initially considered there WAS something wrong with my proposal and that this was a teachable moment I should be grateful for. After all, he seemed as though he knew what he was on about and we had a good rapport. But as I attempted to amend the proposal in a way that he might have found more pleasing, I realised something: I had won literally MILLIONS of dollars of work with that proposal. I liked that proposal a great deal. It was a document I used to support myself, four staff, and my family. That fella's feedback could go in the bin.

Not all feedback is good feedback; we have to consider who it is coming from and how qualified the person is to give feedback, and whether the feedback matches our values and objectives. That's why mentors and communities of business peers are so valuable – they are in a good position to offer informed feedback on your business (as opposed to randoms on LinkedIn). We all know of businesses with a mediocre offering that surprisingly remain functional. I'm sure you want to run a business that's profitable and satisfying. Your 100 Days of Brave journey places you in an advantageous position to do something really special with your life; feel the fear of rejection and do it anyway!

Chapter 31

Everybody needs good networking

Meeting the right people takes a little planning

Feeling a bit tuckered out by all that outwards-looking prospecting and marketing? Know that you need to get out and about to build your business, but feeling shy and as though some structure might do you good? You're right: it will. And that's where networking comes in. Both in real life and online, there are ample opportunities for you to share your service or product with referral partners or new customers.

IRL (in real life) networking

I'll get this out of the way first: structured networking can feel icky and forced. That's why many business networking groups have got such a cultish reputation – each meeting is structured into oblivion and there are KPIs (key performance indicators) out the wazoo. But real-life networking can also be fun, and it is a great way to make new connections, finesse your business skills and begin building a business. Remember how I said that much of a business's success has to do with showing up, time and again? Networking is part of that showing up. Should you hop online, you'll undoubtedly find a ton of formal business networking options.

Here are some hints for networking in real life:

- **Go solo!** I know it can feel scary to meet a group of new people alone, but when networking you want to move beyond your comfort zone. Attending alone means you'll necessarily chat to other business owners.
- **Less is more:** It's fine to have a fistful of business cards ready to go, but don't be that person who is looking over the shoulder of the person they're in conversation with for a better 'mark'. It's yucky. If you have two or three good conversations in a networking session and you can remember what the person you've been speaking with does, you're networking well.
- **Send thank-you cards:** Just like cold prospecting, a thank-you card post-meeting is an unusual and charming gesture. You'll surely be remembered!
- **Be an introducer:** If you see someone looking a little shy on their ownsome, invite them into your conversation. It's polite, and it also positions you as a connector who is generous.

Here are a couple of groups I've had experience with, who they're ideal for and what you can expect from your investment in them.

BNI (Business Network International)

The oldest playa in the book. Word to the wise: BNI is boomer-town. Its ways are from a pre-digital era, and it feels custom-made to work for small-business owners who are blokes. BNI is not inexpensive, and the groups tend to focus on bringing newbie business owners into their fold. So, that's their vibe; I say this as a former BNI member and a guest speaker at many chapters. I have clients who are BNI members who love it and get great business from it.

So, what is BNI? In short, it is a weekly meeting (usually quite early in the morning on a weekday) of a complementary chapter of non-competing professionals. Each week, everyone reminds people of who they are and what they do in a structured 'sharing' session. One member of the chapter has the opportunity to address the group for a longer period of time through a presentation. There's also accountability, with numbers of referrals made within the group calculated, as well as the amount of fees written by the group as a whole within a financial year.

BNI can be an ideal way for startup business owners (in services, particularly) to cut their teeth as networkers. The structure of each meeting means that members slowly finesse their 'elevator' speeches week by week. Is it boring? A bit. Does it help you get some wheels spinning when you've just started? Yes, it can do. It's daggy, but it does have some benefits when you're wanting to leave the house and see other humans regularly, and begin to share your offering with the community.

Fresh Networking

The cool-kids version of BNI – which is to say, only slightly cooler – Fresh Networking (located in Australia) is one of myriad alternative formal business networking clubs. They tend to have fewer demands on time, fewer rules about enforced referrals and more social activities. Ultimately, their regular meetings have a flavour that's similar to BNI: introductions, presentations and sharing. Fresh (and similar alternatives) offer real-world meetings that counter the isolation of startup, and a crew of members who are probably a bit more relaxed than your average BNI bear.

Online

One of the reasons why structured networking is so unfriendly for women is that – at least in contemporary Australia – women are generally the primary caregivers to children. This makes getting out to sparrow-fart early morning meetings very difficult, with evening meetings only just slightly easier. Few networking groups will have physical meet-ups in the middle of the day, claiming that it would eat into productivity and reduce attendee numbers. I personally love a business lunch and so I disagree – but there it is.

Online networking – particularly on Facebook Groups and LinkedIn – is a powerful and wonderful way to connect with others, to toot your own horn and even to meet your entrepreneur peers in real life. Simply search for networking groups relevant to your business or category of service, and you'll soon find hyperproductive communities online. If you're feeling spicy, creating your own online networking community can pay healthy dividends in positive reputation. I created Serious Women's Business: Northside and have brought together a community of around 600 female entrepreneurs. We've held breakfasts and networking events, creek walks and book clubs. (You're welcome to join, by the way.) Primarily this group lives in the digital space, which is democratic, referral-rich and open all hours. Choose one or two online networking groups to invest time in – or better yet, start one in your own area!

BRAVE ACTIVITY: Find your tribe

Take half an hour to explore networking opportunities in your area, or in the digital space. Look to your local council's chamber of commerce, get handy googling or explore Meetup and Facebook

Groups for networking organisations that match your vibe, available time and financial position.

Choose one and participate meaningfully for the following six months. Even if you find that the networking group selected isn't quite your style, you'll meet new people (virtually or in real life), grow your mailing list and finesse your 'elevator speech'. Networking is an ongoing thing when you're in business; try the buffet and see what suits you best. The important thing is that you participate.

Chapter 32

Guerrilla marketing

Go rogue in the best way to
reach your market

Oh boy, do I love 'guerrilla' marketing! When you run a business in startup – or even a mature business that doesn't have a bazillion dollars to spend on television or radio marketing – you need to look for clever communication and advertising solutions. In many ways, the digital economy and our increasing participation in ecommerce and online communication (hello, Zoom meetings!) has democratised marketing.

While we may feel suspicious of Big Data and how our information is being collected and used, as business owners we benefit from being able to target finely segmented customer groups. It's no longer a matter of buying an expensive page in *Vogue* (if you're in retail) or a costly radio advert (if you offer a service) and hoping that you'll tap into the right audience. Business owners have more opportunities for connection AND creativity in this new economy. Here's a variety of unexpected, cost-efficient and impactful ways to market your fledgling or established brand.

Paste-ups, aka rock posters

You know those huge posters advertising gigs on the side of development hoardings, near train stations or in urban laneways? They're an *excellent* way to launch a business, or simply to market in an ongoing way to a local audience. I have done at least four paste-up campaigns, which have been great fun and very cost-effective.

If you run a professional service and not a sexy bar or a swimsuit brand, you might not see the utility of a paste-up campaign. Please, think again! I maintain that paste-up campaigns are also for you! Take my own experience as an example: I run a marketing agency and find that, reputationally, paste-up campaigns are superb for building legitimacy with existing clients and prospects. My clients will send me images of the Ruby Assembly posters they find around town, as this activity obviously makes them feel good about our association, too. When you run a small business, guerrilla marketing is all about bringing the curiosity and the good vibes. Don't demand an unrealistic ROI on this (or any other) guerrilla marketing activity – the idea of a paste-up campaign is brand-building and customer awareness. You won't be able to link your spend back to dollars in sales, but that doesn't mean it isn't effective or helping you to achieve sales. Plus, if you're like me, you'll quite like seeing excellent images of yourself and your brand plastered around town!

Podcast sponsorships

Far less costly and much more targeted than a traditional radio campaign, podcast sponsorships help you connect with a niche target audience. Depending on your relationship with the podcast host, you may even be able to feature as an interview subject on the pod! Don't think that you need to feature your business on top-charting podcasts to be effective: perhaps you could have a month or two's worth of features on a smaller pod that matches with your audience's interests?

Contra exchange

Do you have a client or a supplier you can offer customer exposure or service-in-kind to in exchange for promotion? While I am not often a fan of contra, in some cases it offers valuable access to marketing exposure you'd otherwise find hard to garner. Examples of this could include a pop-up stand promoting your business at a festival or trade show; moving your business to a coworking space in exchange for product or service for a month, giving you exposure to new markets; or even shared shopfront signage, guest speaking opportunities or inclusion in a valuable competition! Contra covers many kinds of non-cash exchanges. Prior to committing to a contra relationship, do all you can to make sure you're getting what you need from the relationship, and that the beginning and conclusion of the arrangement is clear.

Guerrilla branding with merch

So, you're not cashed-up enough to sponsor a networking event or larger festival? Think creatively about how you can align yourself with attendees without too much expenditure. Getting limited amounts of merch made for you and your team is a handy way to rep your brand while out and about. Examples of guerrilla merch include the following:

- **Tees or caps with your logo or hashtag on them:** If your team is attending an industry event, why not get them repping your business? Simple designs are best! I've had success with merch such as t-shirts and hoodies.

- **Photobooths:** When I've sponsored events or had the honour of being a guest speaker at a networking event, I bring the fun in the form of a portable Ruby Assembly photobooth, replete with cute signs and emblems people can hold while having their snaps taken. A small upfront investment means a whole lot of Instagram sharing of my business. How could you do something similar?
- **Wristbands:** Have a Facebook Group you align with your business? Why not get latex wristbands made so members can recognise one another when they're out and about? When suggesting that members or customers wear merch, there must be a compelling reason for them to do so – put a hashtag on one side of the band that aligns with your brand and speaks to their values.

BRAVE ACTIVITY: Going rogue

Spend an hour brainstorming guerrilla marketing opportunities you could pursue for your business and researching potential suppliers and collaborators. Chronicle your findings in your 100 Days of Brave Playbook or business diary.

Chapter 33

Referral relationships

Referrals are the gold-dust of business

From one trusted party to another, a customer referral is a gift. Unlike a new business enquiry from a totally cold prospect, a referral is pre-qualified: a customer has been told about your offering by someone they trust, which makes them MUCH more likely to use your business.

As a newbie business owner, it can be hard to tell qualified referrals from unqualified ones. A QUALIFIED referral is one from a trusted source who understands the needs of the customer, and understands your service. These customers and referral partners are worth going above and beyond for! An UNQUALIFIED referral is from someone you know less well, who has a limited understanding of your business or product and understands only generally the needs of the person they've sent your way.

So, how can you tell one from the other? Time in the game, my friend. The questions that the referred person usually asks will let you know how good of a prospect they are. If they ask about cost immediately, they might not be a great fit. In any case, a good referral is something that needs to be acknowledged. When you receive a referral (qualified OR unqualified), it's important to send a thank-you card. This is usually unexpected and well-received. For qualified referrals, send a gift of gratitude. Good options include a bouquet, a bunch of craft beers, a kilo of coffee, or a book you know the recipient will enjoy. Do this regardless of whether or not they end up doing business with you, as it is the relationship you want to honour. Hopefully in future you'll be able to send clients their way, too.

Should I ask for referral fees?

Whether or not to ask for referral fees is really a personal decision all business owners need to make. I never do; I only refer clients to people I really trust, and what I want most is for my client to receive a wonderful service. I feel like whatever pecuniary interest I get out of a 'deal' only muddies an act of goodwill. I also sense that by not being 'paid' for a referral I get rid of a whole lot of administrivia, and there's a weight of responsibility on the person I'm sending the business to. Some business owners formalise referral relationships, and that's perfectly above board and alright. It's just not my style.

BRAVE ACTIVITY: Thank you for being a friend

Referrals are virtuous circles whose currency is reciprocity. Take an hour to consider the people your customers will most likely need referrals to. If you're a counsellor, you might need a great GP referral, a family lawyer and a psychologist. If you're a personal trainer, you might want to build a connection with a masseuse, a sports physio and a nutritionist. If you're in marketing, you'll want a great graphic designer and web designer on call.

If you don't yet have complementary referral parties in your network, look to build new relationships over coffee. Find out about their service and ideal client so you can better serve your own clients *and* benefit from qualified leads from your fellow business owners.

Chapter 34

Let's start a party up in here

Ring that bell!

And so, my friend, you've made it to the close of Being Brave: Working in and on Your Business. Part Three of 100 Days of Brave is complete, and you're now flying the business plan you've built with your own smart and courageous hands and heart. Congratulations! It's time to have a party.

Do I have to?

For some of you, the idea of throwing a launch party for your biz is delightful! Bringing your nearest and dearest together for a shindig to celebrate your toil and Instagram the shit out of your new venture is a hard-earned reward you've been anticipating. But for many of you, the idea of a party for your biz brings on the anxiety butterflies in your belly. If you're feeling that way, I get it. Here are a few reasons why you might shy away from a business launch, and why you simply must not do so.

Imposter syndrome

Businesses are only successful when people know about them. Since you're just beginning your journey as an entrepreneur, it's possible you're feeling a bit shy or even as though you're an imposter; you might want to keep your project hidden! Please don't. Trust that having gone through this process, you've done 80% more work on shoring up your practice than most people launching a brand. Having worked in startup land and mentored business owners for a decade now, I can guarantee you of this fact. You're ready to share your concept.

Criticism

As we touched on earlier in Part Three of *100 Days of Brave*, learning how to respond to criticism (real or imagined or worried over at 4 a.m.) is part of being in business and doing your own thing. Yes, exposing your idea to the public ventilates it and makes it a potential target for negative feedback. But releasing your biz into the wild also allows it to serve customers and make you money!

Shifting identity

This is probably the biggest reason your unconscious wills you to hide your business away – to not do the podcast, to avoid asking your friends and family to support you, to shy away from Facebook Live sessions or allocating budget to advertising. When you decide to become a business owner, your identity shifts. You become something slightly different to what you were before. If you've had a baby, lost weight, gained weight, married, divorced, dealt with a serious illness, won the lottery or gone bust, you'll know how these events change how you relate to the world and how others relate to you.

When I first began Ruby Assembly, I certainly experienced some flak for the amount of time I was sinking into my new biz from a couple of friends. Our paths were diverging, and our goals and interests were no longer so aligned. I'm happy to say that most of my friendships have survived and flourished as my business has grown. But it's worth acknowledging that spending time on a business or focusing on different aspects of personal growth might change the way you relate to your peers. And that's totally OK. You're not joining a cult, you're trying to become self-sufficient in a strange new world.

Get planning!

So, now we've dealt with any party-related reticence, it is time to get to planning! Whether you've got a big budget for goodie bags and catering, or you're going to keep it on the down low with a few branded items and a fancy spread at home, make sure you invite all those who will support you to join in the celebrations. Make the festivities echo louder by encouraging all who attend to Instagram the bejesus out of the event, and have any merch available and at the ready! Activities you might undertake at your launch party include the following:

· Filming yourself 'launching' your website on your laptop, or projected against a wall
· Pass the parcel, featuring a variety of brand-related merch (or one big brand piece in the middle, with lots of little treats on the way to winning)
· A brand launch playlist that you share with your attendees on their invitation
· Getting your photobooth on, with cute placards that feature your brand and hashtag available for guests to posts with
· A brief launch speech and thank you to attendees for support.

Think about the guest list

Sure, Mum and Dad, the boyf/girlf and besties should be there. But also invite people who've helped you get this far: web designer, graphic designer, lawyer, accountant, your boss (if they've supported your venture), people from networking clubs and people from the business chamber at council, and anyone who runs a coworking space or similar that you might be working from (regularly or occasionally).

Just. Ring. That. Bell.

You've earned it. (Don't forget to tag me in your posts @rubyassembly so I can share your success as well!)

Congratulations! You're now in business. You were brave... and now you're boss.

Closing notes

Well, shit. You've finished *100 Days of Brave*. You took on the challenge, and you were brave for 100 days. That's a serious achievement.

Here's the thing: even if you did not complete the whole 100 Days of Brave in the allotted timeframe, you will be far further along the path to a market-tested, risk-minimised, earnings-optimised business than someone who has not gone through this strategic journey. With business, as with life, we do what we can to the best of our ability. 100 Days of Brave is a roadmap to commercial competency; it's not a guarantee of success, and it cannot replace lived experience in business with all its highs and lows, skirmishes and wins.

I hope that this roadmap has helped you to think differently about the possibility of living life on your own terms, and that it has removed many of the fears you may have held about business. This book is, on one hand, about the nuts and bolts of being an entrepreneur. But more importantly, *100 Days of Brave* is about negotiating a way to reclaim ownership of your identity by building a business that allows you more choice in the everyday – choice to have a family and spend time in a way that serves you, choice to live where you want to most, and choice to build enterprises rich with the values of diversity and inclusion that speak most truly to you.

We are at a turning point in modern industrialised history, where the Dickensian work model of being on-site and 'owned' by your boss no longer functions, where university degrees and the debt they incur may no longer be practical, and indeed may no longer be a guarantee of employment or wealth. You've already shown how brave you're able to be, participating in this 100-day thought experiment and imagining a structured new way of life for yourself, powered by your own business venture.

You can do the thing! I promise you can.

Now's the time to go do it.

P.S. Please keep me in the loop. I want to support your wins and will take care to share them via the 100 Days of Brave Facebook Group and official Instagram @100daysofbrave.

About the author

Iolanthe Gabrie is the Director of Melbourne-based social media agency Ruby Assembly. A senior communications strategist and business mentor, Iolanthe views female business ownership as an essentially empowering feminist act.

Iolanthe is a prolific business writer (iolanthegabrie.com) and podcaster *(Sell Less. Mean More.)*. Her great loves include Eurovision, oracle cards, coworking spaces and fabulous clothing.

Iolanthe lives in Melbourne's north with her husband Yule, daughter Eglė, Wagner the German Shepherd and two villainous cats: Superhans and Baby Billie. She is a very happy lady.

Acknowledgements

Firstly, I want to thank MYSELF for getting this important work DONE. Well done, Iolanthe. You did it, girl!

I began writing *100 Days of Brave* in 2018, during a very different chapter of my life. A divorce, a remarriage, a pandemic and a baby girl later, I was unsure if *100 Days of Brave* would see the light of day. Thankfully, my relentless persistence landed me at my authorial home: Major Street Publishing, under the careful eye of Lesley Williams, editor Will Allen and marketer Eleanor Reader. I'm grateful to this talented trifecta for helping to bring *100 Days of Brave* to life.

I want to acknowledge the support of my friends Elle Steele, Beth Barrett, Breeana Dunbar and Emma Edwards. They witnessed this book grow from a dream into the tome you hold before you, championing the idea and urging me along. Thank you for holding space for me and helping me to realise my potential. I also want to thank my husband Yule Guttenbeil for cheering *100 Days of Brave* to the finish line, and to my parents Elizabeth Gertsakis and Sigi Gabrie for being the best mum and dad around.

Index

Want to connect with Iolanthe, or learn how
you or your organisation might work with her as a
business strategist, social media expert or speaker?

Websites

www.iolanthegabrie.com
www.rubyassembly.com.au

Instagram

@rubyassembly

Podcast

Sell Less. Mean More.

Be better with business books

MAJOR STREET

We hope you enjoy reading this book. We'd love you to post a review on social media or your favourite bookseller site. Please include the hashtag #majorstreetpublishing.

Major Street Publishing specialises in business, leadership, personal finance and motivational non-fiction books. If you'd like to receive regular updates about new Major Street books, email info@majorstreet.com.au and ask to be added to our mailing list.

Visit majorstreet.com.au to find out more about our books (print, audio and ebooks) and authors, read reviews and find links to our Your Next Read podcast.

We'd love you to follow us on social media.

in linkedin.com/company/major-street-publishing

f facebook.com/MajorStreetPublishing

instagram.com/majorstreetpublishing

@MajorStreetPub